photo by Terez Rowley

PETER ROWLEY is a journalist and reviewer of books. His articles and reviews have appeared in *The New York Times Book Review, Saturday Review, New Republic, The Nation,* and *The New Statesman.* He was educated in the United States and England. He and his wife now live in New York City.

NEW GODS
IN
AMERICA

NEW GODS
IN
AMERICA

*An informal investigation
into the new religions
of American youth today*

by
Peter Rowley

DAVID McKAY COMPANY, INC.
New York

NEW GODS IN AMERICA

COPYRIGHT © 1971 BY

Peter Rowley

LIBRARY OF CONGRESS CATALOG CARD NUMBER: 72-165087

MANUFACTURED IN THE UNITED STATES OF AMERICA

FOR TEREZ

*Acknowledgment is made to the following
for permission to reprint copyrighted material.*

"A Universe that Thinks" by Colin Wilson, © 1970 by the *Illustrated London News and Sketch Ltd.,* London. Reprinted by permission.

"The Mystical Experience and the Mystical Commune" by Stanley Krippner, Ph.D., and Don Fersh, courtesy *The Modern Utopian,* Berkeley, Calif.

Short quotes from *The New York Times,* © 1970 The New York Times Company. Reprinted by permission.

Excerpts from *Raja Yoga* by Swami Vivekananda, courtesy the Ramakrishna-Vivekananda Center, New York.

Excerpts from the works of Paul Twitchell, of Eckankar, *The Ancient Science of Soul Travel.* Reprinted by permission of the author.

Excerpts from *Bliss Divine,* pages 357-62, by Swami Sivananda, courtesy The Divine Life Society, Tehri-Garhwal, U.P,. India.

Excerpts from *There Is a River* by Thomas Sugrue, courtesy Holt, Rinehart and Winston, Inc.

"Jai Baba! Hare Krishna, and All That" by Peter Rowley, December 1969, *Madmoiselle* magazine. First published in *Mademoiselle*: © 1969 by The Condé Nast Publications, Inc. Reprinted by permission.

Excerpts from *Discourses,* Volumes 1-3, courtesy Sufism Reoriented, Inc., San Francisco.

Excerpts from *If a Man Asks* by Robert DeGrimston, courtesy The Process Church of the Final Judgment, London.

Excerpts from *SO BE IT*, courtesy The Process Church of the Final Judgment, London.

Excerpts from *Japan's New Buddhism, An Objective Account of Soka Gakkai*, by Kiyoaki Murata, courtesy John Weatherhill, Inc., Tokyo.

Author's Note

This book is a factual account and in most instances the individuals involved, the religions discussed, and the locations concerned are identified by name. In some instances fictitious names are used for individuals and in a few instances the locale in which a described event occurred has been changed. Wherever fictitious names are used this is stated. The name "Followers of Jesus" is not the real name of the religious group described. The name "Ur" is not the real name of the commune described.

CONTENTS

Preface

Part III

AVANT-GARDE CHRISTIAN AND JEW

Part IV

SINO-JAPANESE

PREFACE

The first problem in writing about America's "new religions" is how to define what is "new" and what is "religious." The "religious," I decided, first of all have an element of the unexplainable, or the supernatural or the magical, and second, there must also be some degree of organization, whether it be leaders, rituals, set times for meeting or defined beliefs.

"New" can be "new" in America, but with previous existence in other parts of the world, as well as those beliefs that were invented recently in the U.S. Also, "new" might include religions which have shown dramatic recent growth.

Obviously such criteria will be occasionally inconsistent. Why, for example, have I excluded astrology, which clearly fulfills a quasi-religious function for many? Astrology, however, claims to be a science. Communism, New Thought groups, Rugged Individualism are in a sense religions to many of their advocates, but these seem to me to be regarded more as philosophies. Otherwise this book would wander off into not only social reform but psychoanalysis and whole fields of human activity.

Also, for reasons of space and clarity, this book is limited to the United States, though new religions are popping up in Canada, Australia, England and, so I hear, India (those all-American youngsters from Hare Krishna may already be chanting in Delhi or Bombay).

The purpose of this book is not to study the new Eastern beliefs historically or in terms of comparative religious philosophy or theology. The intention is to present the current facts of this phenomenon—to prove its existence. Will they be a permanent addition to the American religious scene or are they a fad? The conviction of those involved make it certain, it seems to me, that the development of these beliefs in the U.S. will not be transitory. Some of the young have already committed as many as five years of their lives to them.

As for the past, there are countless studies of the thought of Buddhism, Vedanta, Islam, and Christianity, the four main sources for today's new groups. These religions are treated in terms of their current literature, rituals, and members. I have emphasized particularly, where permitted, the character of the participants. Undoubtedly many readers might be tempted, after reading this book, to join one. The personalities of the individuals they will meet are of considerable importance, despite the time-honored or time-worn religious defense, "True, some of our believers have done terrible things in the past, but the beauty and truth of [fill in the appropriate religion] is what's important." However, I attach relevance to the Biblical injunction, "By their fruits ye shall know them."

With very, very few exceptions everyone whom I contacted in connection with this book was cooperative, sometimes exceedingly helpful, usually kind, and often very generous with their time. Viscount Combermere of the University of London and Hayagrivadas of the International Society for Krishna Consciousness graciously read and commented on Chapters I and XIII, but they are of course not responsible for the contents. Certain people were particularly good to me—the ladies of the Meher Baba spiritual center, the members of the Ur Commune, "David Johnson of Aspen, Colorado," Sunja Ackerman, assistant public relations director of Scientology, New York, Mrs. Louise Welch of Gurdjieff, and my agent, Mrs. Carlton Cole. I thank with deep gratitude my editor, Lee Schryver, and my wife, Terez.

LIST OF ILLUSTRATIONS
(following page 112)

PART I

A Variety of Religious Journeys

CHAPTER I

The New Religions

In 1970 about two and a half million people belonged to the new religions of America—Indian, Sino-Japanese, avant-garde Christian and others even more unusual. Ten, twenty, or thirty years ago the total was less than one hundred thousand based on information given me by their disciples, as well as my own observations:

Scientology	600,000
Nichiren Shoshu	200,000
Spiritual Scientists	150,000
Maharishi	125,000
I Ching	125,000
Yoga	125,000
Communes and Organized Hippies	100,000
Black Muslims	100,000
Baha"i'	100,000
Association for Research and Enlightenment	13,000
Meher Baba	7,000
Gurdjieff	5,000
Witchcraft	5,000
Satanic Cults	5,000
Zen	2,000
Subud	1,500

Hare Krishna	1,500
Followers of Jesus	600
The Process Church of the Final Judgment	200

Reports indicate that growth in the latter part of 1970 may be as great as a million people seeking an answer to what seems to them a frightening world; young Americans and some middle-aged and older ones all across the U.S. are joining occult religions or following Eastern and Western gurus and abandoning traditional Christianity and Judaism. A few shave their heads and don saffron robes. Many more increase their self-awareness by meditation, dance, and spirit gatherings. Whether or not the wandering hippie, who hitches a ride from Carmel to San Francisco and who shows an erratic interest in everything except the Establishment, can be classified as religious is a good question. The figures I have given are based mainly on commune members.

The most popular new religion may be Scientology, a blend of psychoanalysis and spirituality. The devotees of *I Ching,* an ancient Chinese book of wisdom, obtain advice by casting coins. Followers of the American psychic-healer Edgar Cayce join in group-therapy-like "Search for God" gatherings in their now nationwide Association for Research and Enlightenment.

In the bizarre, and (who knows?) possibly true religion of Meher Baba, disciples say that this man is God. There is also the highly intellectual, tantalizing and mysterious Gurdjieff-Ouspensky movement, which encourages greater self-awareness. And there are the small (a few thousand followers each) mystical societies such as the Hare Krishna "Back to God" monks, and the equally youthful Spiritual Scientists who see visions and listen to teachers from an immaterial sphere. There is The Process Church of the Final Judgment. There are the Followers of Jesus—basically Roman Catholic minus the Pope, his bishops and churches. There is Subud, founded by Bapak, a living

Indonesian. There is Zen and Yoga and Witchcraft and Baha''i' and the Ur commune, synthesizing the world's old religions into tiny, albeit new groups. In Nichiren Shoshu there is the rubbing of beads and the chanting of "Nam-Myoho-Renge-Kyo" to a scroll upon an altar.

Often immediate conversions, as well as more universal causes, have popularized a sect. Credit the Beatles' interest in the Maharishi and meditation. Credit the underground New-Left poet Allen Ginsberg chanting "Om." Credit the drug gurus like Timothy Leary and his taste for the East. Credit the folk-music heroes like Bob Dylan and Arlo Guthrie, advocates of *I Ching*. However, these were and are catalysts only.

The old religions are unsatisfying to many. Meaningless ritual, adherence to outmoded rules, hypocritical clergy—all of these are charges thrown against Roman Catholicism, Judaism, and Protestantism. The failure of some organized churches to adapt to the time, except for the occasional avant-garde bishop (such as the late James Pike) or priest (like the poet Dan Berrigan), has left the young with little alternative but to seek elsewhere. Drugs, with their inherent threat to health and concentration on selfish sensation, fail also. And the hippie movement with its too-formless emphasis on love.

The sweep to new mysticisms, magic, and supernatural theories certainly owes much to the confusion and danger confronting us today. Universities often seem overwhelmingly monstrous and machinelike, and corporations even more so. There is social unrest, demonstrations and riots, and death in Vietnam. There is air and water pollution ranging from atomic particles to industrial wastes. And there is always the vision of someone pressing a button in a military installation and blowing everything up. Small wonder that some meaning is sought within the self, to explain the whole and to counteract the turmoil of frustration and danger. Much of America—cities, airports, and highways—is visually dismaying: endless neon signs, gas sta-

tions, telephone poles, used-car lots, smoke, factories, decay
and noise, commercialism run rampant, the anarchy of free
enterprise, the "buck," "Making it." Gallup, Arizona, an
Indian town, is a garish replica of most white cities. Telephone lines cross once-perfect valleys. Houses jumble on
cliff sides, mountainsides, slope sides—thrown up with no
regard for the terrain or the neighbor. It is like a nineteenth-century Rube Goldberg machine—a large part of the
U.S. today—gone mad. Plasticized food. Muzak. Fake English cocktail bars. Gaudy Italian pizzerias. This as much as
anything else has caused the withdrawal of the young and
the disgust of the more sensitive middle-aged.

The new religions encompass science and reduce prag-
matic research to an aspect of the universe rather than
combatting Darwinian thought as traditional Christianity
and Judaism have done. Dr. Margaret Mead has written,
"The young have turned to Asian religions in which doc-
trines of reincarnation have elevated the position of all living things, however minute, to possible embodiment of past
or future human souls . . .

"In this turn away-or-back for models, we can recognize
two potentialities: 1. the development of an eclectic world-
wide ethic of conservation that will include not only the
Judeo-Christian ideas of man given dominion over nature,
of man as custodian of God's world and thus taking a latter-
day part in creation, but also the ideas of the other conti-
nents, the outcome of which might be among other things
vegetarianism; or 2. an entirely new synthesis between religion and science . . .

"We need a religious system with science at its very
core."

In *The Illustrated London News,* June 20, 1970, Colin
Wilson said: "What is happening is this. For more than two
hundred years, science and philosophy have tended to be
materialistic. There is a story of Goethe and Schiller coming out of a scientific meeting in Jena. They had just met
for the first time. Goethe hated the materialistic attitude of

the scientists, and said to Schiller: 'There ought to be some other way of grasping nature—as *active and living* . . .' Schiller shrugged and said: 'That's not scientific. It's just an *idea* of yours.' For two hundred years, science has agreed with Schiller. And now, amazing as it seems, it is beginning to agree with Goethe." Wilson then cited Dr. L.S.B. Leakey's observation of the flattid bugs who can form a beautiful imitation flower as evidence of mind-affecting genes. "It is the scientists themselves who are slowly conceding that things are more complicated than they thought." He pointed out that our genes are "coded" like a computer. "An acorn is a 'programme' of an oak tree: But who-or-what programmes the computer?" Wilson concluded, "I predict that by the year 2000, the rigid scientific materialism of the nineteenth century will be regarded as a thing of the past, an interesting and necessary phase in human development—just as the rigid, narrow, religious code of the Jews has been a vital phase in the development of man's religious consciousness. But I think it will also be regarded with mild wonder and amusement, as one of the more preposterous manifestations of the human spirit."

Geographically, the followers of the new religions are everywhere in the U.S., but strongest on the East and West Coasts. The Midwest and Central states seem the least interested. Big cities are favored, but Corpus Christi, Texas, has been visited by the Maharishi's movement. University communities are fertile ground for seeds from the East.

A very large number, if not the majority, of the young joining these beliefs have had less than satisfactory experiences with their parents. Middle-aged parents, influenced by materialism and memories of the Depression, either ignored their children or held them in rigid psychological chains. Many new beliefs and particularly the communes are new "families" replacing those that never existed. The elderly Yogis, the Gurdjieff leaders in their sixties, the leader of the Followers of Jesus, and "Bapak" are clearly father-figures, substituting for those "Dads" who gave their time to the corporation rather than to their sons or daughters. Thus the rebellion of these young joined forces with small bands of older people who had carefully nurtured Eastern religions over the decades. The elderly women of Meher Baba, and "Mrs. Welch" of Gurdjieff became mother-figures.

The membership of these sects is almost exclusively middle- and upper-income. With the exception of the Black Muslims and Baha''i', there are very few blacks involved. A number of those in the Gurdjieff Foundation come from educated, well-off families with inherited income. Some black Hare Krishna adherents are of low-middle-income background although the movement is primarily middle-class.

Scientology is almost the only new native American religion and it has spread across the Atlantic. Nichiren Shoshu, though Japanese, is very "main street," (drum majorettes, etc.), in its approach.

The growth of these new religions must be costing the traditional ones many a potential minister, priest, or nun. A thousand young men and women are of equivalent rank in the Krishna group.

Edward Gibbon in *The Decline and Fall of the Roman Empire* wrote, "the various modes of worship which prevailed in the Roman Empire were all considered by the people as equally true; by the philosophers as equally false; and by the magistrate as equally useful . . . Rome, the capital of a great monarchy, was incessantly filled with subjects and strangers from every part of the world, who all introduced and enjoyed the favorite superstitions of their native country. Every city in the empire was justified in maintaining the purity of its ancient ceremonies; and the Roman senate, using the common privilege, sometimes interposed to check this inundation of foreign rites, . . . But the practice of superstition is so congenial to the multitude that, if they are forcibly awakened, they still regret the loss of their pleasing vision. Their love of the marvelous and supernatural, their curiosity with regard to future events, and their strong propensity to extend their hopes and fears beyond the limits of the visible world, were the principal causes which favoured the establishment of Polytheism."

There was said to have been a dramatic increase of interest in the occult in Imperial China just prior to the collapse of the Manchu Dynasty. University students wore their hair long as a protest against Chinese society. A similar phenomenon existed in Germany immediately after the First World War—in the turmoil of the early days of the Weimar Republic.

The rise of communes occurred in mid-nineteenth century America. Thoreau, then as now, was influential, and Emerson's transcendentalism—with its turn toward the East—may have presaged today's development. Early signs of it appeared in the writings on religion of the English critic, Matthew Arnold, and the Christian Science Church with its emphasis on spirituality, science, and the unreality of the material world may be a forerunner.

The movement is generally conservative, in that it may distract left-wing political activity. But it can also be argued that such conversion strengthens the character of those involved and makes them more effective for left-wing political activity. Most of them hold left-wing political views, and Hare Krishna monks, for example, have participated in many anti-Vietnam demonstrations. One way of opposing the Army is through a religious exemption. The young in Hare Krishna and the Followers of Jesus receive deferments.

All of the new groups are more strict concerning sex than the "free love" ethos of the hippies, the world from which many came to their new beliefs, usually cutting their hair and taking jobs in the process. Freer, more enthusiastic rituals offer a clear-cut challenge to the established churches. Musically, George Harrison of the Beatles has produced a "Hare Krishna" song. The rock opera, "Tommy," by *The Who* was inspired by Meher Baba. Arlo

Guthrie says the *I Ching* has influenced his songs in a minor way. Bob Dylan has promoted the *I Ching*. In a parallel development *The New York Times* reported, ". . . rock music has got religion." A number of popular songs such as "Oh Happy Day" by the Edward Hawkins singers and "Jesus is Just Alright" by The Byrds have appeared. The Electric Prunes and another group, Spooky Tooth, have recorded "Mass in F Minor" and "Ceremony: An Electronic Mass," respectively. The Moody Blues have issued "Aum," inspired by Eastern religions. The Coven sing a "black mass." The Bob Seger System's album is titled "Lucifer." United Artists' LP is "A Satanic Happening."

The artist Peter Max was one of two people who persuaded Swami Satchidananda to come to America.

Most of these new religions encourage varying forms of vegetarianism.

In the traditional Christian churches the new theology of hope could be said to represent a turn toward the supernatural and away from the material.

A mark of these times is the waning of the Horatio Alger myth in the American way of success. The increasing difficulty of the individual to stand up against big government, big labor, and big business, and the greater obstacles to riches must be influencing some of the young to turn to more personal inner searches. The innocence of America internationally is no longer credible, as American capital expansion, growing steadily overseas after World War II, disenchants some citizens. To them the world of the spirit is more inviting than that of the State Department or the Pentagon.

The New York Times, August 26, 1970, in a long article described the research of Robert E. L. Masters and Jean Houston, directors of the Foundation for Mind Research in Manhattan, which uses scientific equipment on a number of subjects. Dr. Masters is a former philosophy teacher, and Miss Houston earned a doctorate in the philosophy of religion from Columbia University. They "concluded that ordinary people can have profound religious experiences like those of the great Eastern and Western mystics, without the use of drugs."

CHAPTER II

Baha''i'

The Baha''i' Faith has doubled its membership in the last
ten years—notably among the young and blacks in the
South. Membership may be one hundred thousand. The
prophet-founder was a nineteenth-century persecuted
Persian, Baha'u'lla'h. His son, who died in 1921, carried the
faith to America. It claims to be a universal religion, uniting all others, its founder "God," and it emphasizes world
peace and other admirable goals with a few odd little quirks
such as banning alcohol, monasticism, and cremation.
Arnold Toynbee has compared Baha''i''s growth to that of
Christianity in the Roman Empire, Baha''i' to be possibly
the religion of the world unity in the future. (See Arnold J.
Toynbee, *A Study of History,* Vol. VII, and Arnold J.
Toynbee, *Christianity Among the Religions of the World,*
1957.)

Colonel Salvatore Pelle, Director of information for
Baha''i' in the U.S. at their Wilmette, Illinois, national
headquarters, says, "We have doubled in the past ten years
the number of our assemblies to five hundred and nineteen." (Each Baha''i' community has a local assembly of
nine or more members. I estimate about two hundred members per assembly because Baha''i' refuses to give its membership per head, only by the number of assemblies.)

"The growth has been spectacular in certain areas—one

quarter of our new converts are in California. There has been rapid growth in greater Chicago and surrounding states, the New York area, and very recently in the deep South—Louisiana, Georgia, Mississippi, and the Carolinas —where the newcomers are ninety-nine percent black. [There is a parallel here between the spread of integration in the South's schools, restaurants and public parks and Baha''i''s appeal to all races.] In the past ten years there has been a steady increase in youths under twenty-five, some years this group increases more than the adult growth."

In a black middle-income suburb of Atlanta I was welcomed into a Sunday morning meeting of the local Assembly. Of the eight members present, five were under forty. All were school teachers, several with higher degrees, and only the two older women were white. Most were married with children. This was the Atlanta Spiritual Assembly. Before I entered the pleasant middle-income house, I saw a white cop giving a black a speeding ticket.

Lillian: "So glad I'm not black." She had brown skin.

Neeka: "I heard about Baha''i' from the lady across the street. . . . She said things like 'member of the faith'. . . . I was a Baptist . . . I was disenchanted with the minister . . . He made some remarks . . . Evangeline gave me some literature . . . I called the Better Business Bureau and the F.B.I. to find out if it was a subversive organization because I thought this multi-racial thing was too good to be true."

Alyce: "After a search of four years I found Baha''i'. I was a member of a Christian Church. I had not found real identity. I met two persons, white, through sit-ins, who were sympathetic. Their spirit was not the conversion type or saying they liked Negroes, but there was something about them. This was in Augusta [There was a slight laugh because Augusta, Georgia, was under martial law that day.] They demonstrated what they believed in. I didn't get the same old crud about 'how I played with Negroes as a child' . . . They said come over to their house instead of coming to yours as whites usually did . . . They demonstrated their oneness."

Miriam: "Christians were always anti-Islam. In Baha"i' I learned the Christians were the 'baddies' in the Crusades."

One of the new Baha"i' groups is in Dawson, Georgia, a small rural town. It was started by a black couple who gave up a job at four dollars and seventy-five cents an hour in Louisiana to move to Dawson as "pioneers," the Baha"i' term for missionaries, finally getting a job at one dollar an hour after a six-month search. There are now "one hundred to one hundred and fifty" members in Dawson, almost all blacks. Many of them are workers in a peanut factory.

The multi-racialism was more evident at a Saturday night "social" in New York City where there were Puerto Ricans, blacks, Jews, Anglo-Saxons, a man who looked like an Italian, and a Pole or Russian from the Columbia Business School. Generally speaking, they were of a low-income or lower-middle-income level.

The pretty little Puerto Rican girl Denys, who works for Bell Telephone, expressed the same belief as the recent Roman Catholic teaching on sex (how often had I read such arguments in Roman Catholic pamphlets): "Premarital sex is not a good idea because of the danger of an accident. Also you might pick up something—a disease. Then a girl makes an emotional attachment and when it breaks up she's hurt. If you haven't done it before marriage, it's special." This is one of the tenets of Baha"i'.

In Harlem we watched rhythmic, sexy, lithe young dancers do African dances for the entertainment of people at Harlem Prep and a few Baha"i' followers (nine or so of the teachers there are Baha"i'). Riding back on the subway, a white truck driver-machinist who might have been Italian or part Persian, said, "I was a Catholic but now I prefer Baha"i'. I like to travel and work in different parts of America." He had funny hand and forearm motions when talking, and his brown eyes seemed slightly glazed and liquid. Afterward at the Baha"i' "social" he sat alone.

There was a dreadful lonely old woman, a long-time Baha"i' member, who talked my head off throughout the evening.

At a Sunday service a chiropractor, about sixty years old, told me, "For three years my wife, daughter, and I lived in Switzerland, starting Baha"i' there. They're in Florida now as pioneers to spread Baha"i', have been for three years. I can't sell my practice in the New York area, but talk with them on phone, three times this week, and write."

Pioneers! I had visions of these very ordinary-looking middle-class Americans amidst all those white-stucco Florida suburbs living in their imaginations the world of the prophet Baha'u'llu'h and spreading their beliefs to all the others in those sun-glittering developments.

"Fireside Meetings," or small gatherings in private homes, are one of the principal Baha"i' activities. It was a pleasant living room in an apartment in Queens, a respectable, well-lit area with middle-income shops. The Taraz's apartment (he is a dentist from Iran) was decorated with a few Oriental rugs, ornamental dishes, and a number of Baha"i' photos (delegates gathered before temples). The temple in the U.S., the Baha"i' "House of Worship," in Wilmette, Illinois, is a beautiful Mosque-type structure; the concrete "fabric" is so delicate it looks like lace.

On my arrival Dr. Taraz had said, "In Iran we had 20,000 martyrs in the nineteenth century."

Joan (as I shall call her), an elderly married woman with a middle-class American accent and gray hair, a pleasant roundish face, had been imported from outside of Queens to tell me and the others of spreading the Baha"i' Faith in Africa.

Joan declared, "We noticed how the natives in Africa without any material benefits were much more spiritual than Americans."

Dr. Taraz wondered, "Is it the cities that make us so suspicious, particularly on the East Coast?"

He then said to a casually dressed young man, a medical doctor, who was slouched on a settee, "Of course you could go to a village in an underdeveloped country."

Staring at his feet Doctor "Y" replied, "I would not be

able to use my medical skills because of the lack of equipment. I would be reduced to first aid."

Joan asserted, "You could build a medical center there." This may have been her opening salvo to persuade Doctor "Y" to become a "pioneer." The doctor probably came from a hard-working Jewish family, worked his way through medical school, and now wanted to enjoy the fruits of his labors. Gambia or anywhere else in Africa did not sound very inviting to him.

She then launched into a long, long discourse on the virtues of spiritual life, Baha"i', and experiences in Africa. Filled with platitudes, it almost put me to sleep.

In fact Doctor "Y" went to sleep. His wife, a pretty young thing with a rather horselike face and red scratched areas on her knees, woke him, obviously embarrassed, and had a whispered conference with Dr. Taraz.

"My husband had the cartilege removed from his knee," she said. "He's not feeling well."

Joan continued. By 11 P.M. (the "Fireside" had started at 8:30 P.M.) it suddenly struck me that the others were not bored at all. They were the bearers of hidden truth, the members of a divine club. To me what was the dreariest tidbit was to them a message of supreme wisdom rippling across the world.

Before I left, an Italian-American girl with frizzy black hair, red lips and ample thighs, said intensely, "I declared two weeks ago. I signed a card saying I believed. It took me five years to get over my Catholic background. In the Catholic school, which I taught in this year to be quite sure I understood what I was leaving, I was at a teacher's meeting at noon. You're supposed to say an obligatory prayer in Baha"i'. I couldn't remember it and so had to look in my bag at the little prayer book half-opened without being seen. The others must have wondered why I kept looking in my bag."

Dr. Taraz's friend, Dr. Fuller, the old chiropractor, said, "Everyone here came from considerable distances—ten, twenty miles."

The many Baha"i' publications seemed to me notable for their boring, if elevating, contents. Perhaps this is the result of being a universal religion necessitating a common denominator quality whose worthwhile moral precepts can cover every cult. In *The Seven Valleys and The Four Valleys* by Baha'u'lla'h, however, the introduction by a later commentator contains several sharp points:

"Men have placed their trust in the false gods of racialism, nationalism, and communism, and they have spurned the God of love, justice and mercy."

"World War II supplied the spectacle of Protestants fighting Protestants and Catholics killing Catholics."

Baha"i'"s first woman martyr saying to her captors in the nineteenth century, "You can kill me as soon as you like, but you cannot stop the emancipation of women."

The Hidden Words of Baha'u'lla'h, comprised of eighty-two holy sayings, "is to be identified with the Hidden Book of Fatimah," disclosed by the Angel Gabriel as a consolation to Muhammad's daughter grieving over her Father's death. This tiny book is also sleep-inducing.

The Baha"i' hope that God "will send unto us His Holy Manifestations . . . great world prophets" (from *The Divine Art of Living*) is similar to Baba's statement of being the latest Incarnation of the Deity.

Two books, copyrighted by The New History Foundation, now possibly out-of-print, (*Broken Silence* and *From Gaslight to Dawn*) show that in the early Forties Baha"i' was involved in a lawsuit between the organization and two ex-members, though still believers, over the right to use the name "Baha"i'." The two dissident Baha"i's won the case in the Appellate Court of New York State. Col. Pelle claims that subsequently, court decisions granted the National Spiritual Assembly the right to use the term Baha"i' exclusively, and has denied others who wished to form groups legal permission to do so. The new universal religion may not appear—in its demand for exclusivity—quite so universal as one might have hoped. But the Faith had to be preserved as it was, no doubt.

CHAPTER III

Gurdjieff

One of the most intellectually tantalizing religious groups are the Gurdjieff-Ouspensky disciples. Gurdjieff, about whom much gossip and many facts have emerged, was a powerful-personality Russian philosopher, who died in Paris in 1949. "Gurdjieff was better on emotions; Ouspensky, a mathematician-disciple, on theory," said Ellen Silverman of Los Angeles, who has a yogalike calm and wears her hair in enormous pigtails. Today, their philosophy of inner development is attracting untold numbers to its gatherings of talk, dance, and music, despite their de-emphasis of proselytization.

There are two groups of Gurdjieff people—those from the Gurdjieff Foundation and disciples of W. A. Nyland, who is believed to live near Warwick in the State of New York. Figures are hard to obtain, but there are about four hundred active participants in the New York area belonging to the Foundation. It also has groups in Los Angeles, San Francisco, Toronto, Montreal, Boston, and Cleveland. Guessing Nyland's total, five thousand should not be too far off. Gurdjieff's books, according to the Foundation and the owner of the leading occult book store in New York City, have had very considerable sales recently. With the exception of a woman leader, I was consistently and continually blocked from a penetrating study of the movement. I was not allowed to see their Eastern-inspired dancing (though I was told I might be able to see this at another time), attend more than one carefully pre-arranged group meeting, learn more than the most rudimentary (and even that not always) details of their organization, and was even urged "not to read *All and Everything*."

From the ten Gurdjieff people I talked with, I have a tentative impression that a number of them are the opposite of Gurdjieff himself, who appears to have been a full-blown character, whereas they appear shy. The reluctance to disclose their activities seems to stem also from the elusive quality of the comfortably-off (though many are not, I am told) and an understandable desire not to have Gurdjieff's ideas corrupted by simplistic reports. There is an eerie quality noticeable about some of the Gurdjieff people some of the time.

Colin Wilson, the author of *The Outsider*; P. L. Travers, who wrote the Mary Poppins books; Kathryn Hulme of *The Nun's Story*; and Katherine Mansfield, the noted short story writer, have all been interested in Gurdjieff.

In a lilting, convinced voice, Ellen, a Montessori teacher, twenty-three, said she and her friends did not like to talk about G-O, as G-O was life, and talking about G-O was withdrawing from life. Ellen's group in Los Angeles consists mainly of young people in the arts and professions, and there are Gurdjieff followers at Harvard, Yale, Radcliffe, and Sarah Lawrence.

In New York, twelve young (almost all Ivy Leaguers or graduates of same) assemble under the guidance of a doctor's wife, Mrs. Louise Welch. George Thompson (not his real name), is twenty-four, (Yale, '67), a gentle young man with a wave of blond hair and a bony face. He is earning a doctorate at Columbia in philosophy. Mary, twenty-two, his wife of two months, is confident—a pretty blonde, similarly soft in manner, who completed her bachelor's degree this year at the University of California. Also present was the other older member of their group, an editor who asked not to be identified.

George: "I was an Ivy League hippie, taking a lot of drugs, wore huge sideburns [he's now clean-shaven], took a lot of acid, and was planning to take STP until I encountered Gurdjieff. I was interested in states of consciousness, mysticism, and had previously worked out an epistemology for religion and art. Then, at Yale, I met a young friend who introduced me to Gurdjieff. Gurdjieff, I realized, was simple, obvious, and direct, a more real kind of life, solid. It releases the imagination in higher emotional centers. In drugs I couldn't be sure what was real. With Gurdjieff, I see that our life doesn't belong to us now. We have to reclaim it."

Mary: "I have some hesitation in saying Gurdjieff is God. Each person discovers the truth in himself differently. We're not limited by dogma; you can only believe in things you can verify yourself. In the *Duino Elegies* of Rilke, one realizes that the whole idea is hope, that one realizes one's life. Gurdjieff's idea is that as we are, we experience no reality, such as my emotions and thoughts, and he doesn't promise happiness at the beginning."

George: "It's like the medieval paintings of the soul on the man's shoulder. We want another self to watch oneself."

Mary: "It's being aware of my anxieties right now."

George: "You do not dump the bad things. Sometimes it's better to be uptight. Sometimes you can't control your negative emotions. Nothing's obvious. Everything can be turned upside down."

Mrs. Welch: "All religions are the same, in essence."

George: "Gurdjieff is not a belief or a religion."

Mary: "Gurdjieff is an understanding, not a technique."

George: "Mary and I try to ask each other at the end of the day what the day has brought us. We read *All and Everything or Beelzebub's Tale to His Grandson* [by Gurdjieff] aloud. There are no sacred texts."

Mary: "Mrs. Welch rephrases your questions, asks you what you are really asking. In our group, we don't dance. Others do. There are exercises, not for audiences but for the participants, for their self-study."

George: "The churches are not powerhouses of spiritual energy any more."

Mrs. Welch: "Gurdjieff work should be taken seriously or not at all. We would not want to see it a fad or fashionable. You might call it esoteric Christianity. Gurdjieff is a form of deep acceptance of life, not resignation."

Some of the Gurdjieff people have an infuriating way of leading one on and then suspending one in mid-air. The most frustrating interview of my life was four hours with Lord Pentland, the president of The Foundation, and a young woman follower, when he managed to reply to my questions with an extraordinary number of non-answers. Fictionalized, but representative, the conversation went as follows: if I said, "God is good," he would reply, "It depends."

"It depends on what?"

"God."

"You mean God isn't all good?"

"I didn't say that."

Lord Pentland, the St. Paul of the movement in America, is an Englishman, probably in his later fifties, who can be charming. The reader may wish to compare Lord Pentland's approach to me and Gurdjieff's treatment of visitors described later on.

"Gurdjieff," according to Larry Morris, another early disciple, "chose Lord Pentland to head the work in America." A profound believer in Gurdjieff's ideas, John Pentland told my wife he had moved to the U.S. some years ago expressly for this purpose, and I had the feeling that otherwise he found America slightly distasteful. A close friend of Pentland says that actually he loves this country.

The Gurdjieff work (The Gurdjieff people always refer to what they do, as Gurdjieff himself did, as "the work") is centered at a town house on East Sixty-third Street in New York owned by the Gurdjieff Foundation. Said Morris, "I'd rather not tell you who the secretary and treasurer are, as it would give more of an impression of organization than is justified." Here are kept Gurdjieff's writings, as well as

books on religions of the world. Classes and sacred dances
are conducted here. In Westchester County the Foundation
owns a thirty-acre property. On weekends they do pottery,
weaving, and other artistic activities.

Lord Pentland flies once a month or so to Los Angeles
and San Francisco where he heads groups. Mr. Morris, a
retired cultural attaché of the U. S. State Department, leads
groups in Boston and Cleveland. Mrs. Welch flies to hers in
Toronto.

"W. A. Nyland," according to Morris, "lectures and leads
followers. He used to be connected with the Foundation."

"Other people," says Morris, a courtly, reserved, gray-
haired man, "read the books, see that they can make something of it and start groups."

I was given a tour through the Gurdjieff Foundation
building on East Sixty-third Street. Few, if any, outsiders
have ever been inside. There was a large hall painted a
cheerful off-white where the "sacred dances and movements" are performed. But I did not see them, though I was
told that films have been shown in New York. The last
public performance was given about ten years ago. Upstairs
were various lounge-type meeting rooms. One was one-half
or one-third the size of the gymnasium-type hall. Mr. Morris said, "The whole New York group fitted in there a few
years ago but now we need the large hall."

I had an exciting, mysterious glimpse of a youngish man
meditating in a sort of Oriental trance. That was it! Except
for the downstairs office. Mrs. Welch says, "Trances are definitely *not* encouraged in the Gurdjieff work. We are interested in *waking up,* and not in any form of day or night
dream." Morris said, "I do not think you can write about
Gurdjieff successfully unless you join as a sincere disciple.
Otherwise you cannot attend the meetings."

Beelzebub's Tales to His Grandson, the first of three
books under the general title of *All and Everything,* is 1238
pages long, costs $9.95, and is an infuriatingly written book
because of its convolutions of sentences and hodgepodge of
subjects.

The second book, *Meetings with Remarkable Men,* is a

remarkable book. Its conclusion is, "Formerly it may be said, my whole being was possessed by egoism. All my manifestations and experiencings flowed from my vanity. The meeting with Father Giovanni killed all this, and from then on there arose in me that 'something' which has brought the whole of me to the unshakable conviction that, apart from the vanities of life, there exists a 'something else' which must be the aim and ideal of every more or less thinking man, and that it is only this something else which may make a man really happy and give him real values, instead of the illusory 'goods' with which in ordinary life he is always and in everything full."

The secrets of this "something else" will be revealed presumably in "the third series of my writings," so far unpublished. Though Gurdjieff refers to this third book a number of times and the foreword says it is "being prepared for publication," a question about it addressed to a Gurdjieff leader, produced a vague answer.

For the most part *Meetings* is a succession of chapters about "remarkable" personalities Gurdjieff knew and collaborated with in searches for the meaning of life. Their adventures are exciting: a camel bite leads to death, escape from "white slavery," disguises, dervishes, fights, and desert and mountainous treks through many dangers. Gurdjieff tells a good story.

Orage says in his Translators' Note: "Gurdjieff was a master. . . . But to meet him was always a test. In his presence every attitude seemed artificial. Whether too deferential, or on the contrary pretentious, from the first moment it was shattered; and nothing remained but a human creature stripped of his mask and revealed for an instant as he truly was." Gurdjieff writes, "From my point of view, he can be called a remarkable man who stands out from those around him by the resourcefulness of his mind, and who knows how to be restrained in the manifestations which proceed from his nature, at the same time conducting himself justly and tolerantly towards the weaknesses of others."

In the book Gurdjieff "managed to earn a great deal,

having besides my official salary several unofficial sources of
income of a rather questionable character." These he describes as payment by local officials to "arrange" the laying
of a new railroad through their towns. Whereas Gurdjieff
had no such power, as assistant to a railroad engineer, he
knew of its route beforehand. On another occasion: "At the
house I asked the landlady for scissors, clipped my sparrow
to the shape of a canary, and then colored it fantastically
with the aniline dyes. I took this sparrow to Old Samarkand
where I immediately sold it, claiming that it was a special
'American canary.' " He sold a number of such sparrows
and fled before discovery. A Gurdjieff expert says these in-
cidents should be considered as "parables, an Eastern form
of writing."

In a secret monastery he observed "sacred dances" which
he says he might describe "in a special book." Were these
the model for the sacred dances currently performed by the
Gurdjieff people?

Chapters V to VIII of *The Master Game* by Dr. Robert S.
DeRopp are highly interesting. These pages describe the
current "work" of The Gurdjieff Foundation in the study
of man, the Universe and its mysteries, according to its
leaders. The book has frequent witty asides, historical
commentaries, and sharp observations on men and women,
ranging from power-mad conquerors to banal hippies. It's
not entirely original ("Some truths can't be original," re-
plies Mrs. Welch).

Dr. DeRopp, a biochemist, outlines the three principal
physical classifications—endomorphs, mesomorphs, and
ectomorphs—and their corresponding temperments—
viscerotonic, somatotonic and cerebrotonic. He describes
the essences of men and their play-acting selves. He describes where psychotherapy has to stop and creative psychology begin. He emphasizes the five stages of consciousness. The third, and most familiar, "self-sense is narrow,
limited and strictly personal." The objective of the guru
and the student—the fifth—is the transcendence of self.

CHAPTER IV

Subud

The sign in the valley of Carmel said: SUBUD-CALI-FORNIA. It was a sunny afternoon. The late spring wheat had been cut and was lying in golden ribbons on the fields. Horses and ponies grazed in the valley between the moun-tainsides. The air was cool, yet the sun was warm.

Inside was a hall with hemp matting on the floor, the walls bare except for a photo of Bapak. In the adjacent small office was a young man in blue jeans.

He said reticently, "I cannot answer your questions. I will bring someone else."

Emerging from another door were a short friendly-faced young man and a woman who was wearing a long blue kimono with long brown hair tied behind with a brown ivory-type clasp, and brown eyes. Her age was indeterminate but was perhaps forty.

"What is your practice?" I said.

"Subud is an experience."

"Can you describe it?"

The young man paced up and down on the rope carpet-ing.

"Every person has a different experience," she said. "Mr. John Bennett wrote *Towards Subud* and said three months afterward he regretted it. The experience changes every minute." I knew John Bennett had written a work on this religion.

"Can you tell me of an experience, say, your last one?"

She paused, first she smiled. Then her jaw muscles worked. We waited for an answer for several long minutes.

Her voice broke. "Before Subud I would say something but it was not real. My last experience was to feel real, to know it was I who communicated. Latihan comes to a person. It can happen in the company of the more experienced, the helpers, but it does not come from them."

At the beginning she had said, "Many Gurdjieff people come to Subud."

What is Subud? In terms of numbers the lady in the Carmel Center estimated there were two thousand members in America. This woman and another source spoke of Subud groups in Los Angeles, San Francisco, Chicago, Washington, Denver, Phoenix, Boston, and New York. Jacob Needleman, chairman of the Philosophy Department at San Francisco State College, in his interesting book, *The New Religions,* says there are about seventy Subud centers in America. The North American headquarters is in Los Angeles, of course.

The founder of Subud is Bapak, who is Indonesian. Muhammad Subuh was called Bapak, the Indonesian term of respect for an elderly man. The essence of Subud is "Latihan," a form of inner awakening during which the sources of life, or God, enter the soul.

The Carmel Valley center has about forty members. This group was started in 1958 by the English disciple, Bennett. Bapak himself visited at that time.

Earlier in the spring I interviewed a mid-European member of Subud in his apartment in New York. However, at that time I could understand little of what I had heard. The following is written from my notes at the time of the interview.

"God originated Subud by Bapak. After a thousand days he understood, having a Subudian experience every day of the thousand. If he went to a party he did not want to be different from everyone else, but still he went on and on in Subud.

"Bapak is still living and will be in the U. S. next August, but will only see Subud people. At first a disciple of Guru, then of Bapak . . . Roiphe, a linguist, part Lebanese, part English, is also still alive, but lives in different places, usually teaching.

"Roiphe went to London about 1958, attracting a number of English people. He met John Bennett there, the English Gurdjieff leader, and introduced Bennett to Subud. Then other Gurdjieff people turned to Subud.

"We do Latihan, which means 'exercises' in Indonesian . . . we try not to think when we do this or use our feelings. In this moment when we stop thinking and feeling, our inner life or our soul is somehow in contact with the life force. . . .

"A majority of us are under forty, mainly artistic and intellectual, many painters, artists, writers, teachers, simple workers, taxi drivers, and actors. I am a motion picture cameraman. . . ."

Latihan is the purpose of Subud. The idea is to be open to God's power. When in Latihan, one is fully conscious and can end it any time. It is said not to be a trance or hypnosis. A pamphlet available at the Carmel Valley center describes Latihan as an "inner vibration," says it shows itself physically at first, and then sinks ever deeper into the psyche. Students of comparative religions may see a similarity in the Subudian experience and the speaking in tongues described in Chapter XVII. Needleman maintains that Latihan is freeing one of one's animal energies by the infusion of higher forces, i.e. God. Latihan can mean love to one person, incredible freedom to another, something either very heavy, light, powerful, or nothing to other individuals.

The woman at the Carmel office said the Latihan meetings are held with the sexes separate. They take place twice a week for half an hour. Initiates must wait three months

before doing Latihan. Apparently a newcomer senses powers entering into him. One psychologist, sitting outside,
compared it to the way he felt before marrying. A helper is
employed to channel Latihan to a beginner.

Behavior at Latihan meetings is diverse. Though one can
do it alone, it is better done in a group. Persons present can
vary in numbers from a few to several hundred. One expert
on American religions told me, "Some people are very
powerfully attracted to Subud. Some people have changed
their whole personality, acting very strangely."

One should take off one's watch, eyeglasses and take out
of one's pockets any hard objects. One should relax with
hands hanging by the sides and not think. Evidently some
new people can last as long as six months without feeling
Latihan. Individuals, who await Latihan calmly, can walk
or sit or jump or shout or dance or sing. The sounds emanating from a Latihan meeting can be like a siren quietly
humming or chanting or singing without words or jungle-
like cries. Sometimes the sound is beautiful. One man said
the forces from above were so strong he wound up on the
floor. He compared his experience with God to that of
Moses. The members look quite unruffled when emerging
from the hall after Latihan.

Typically there are reports of cures, including the saving
of the life of a European movie star's baby, disappearance
of disease, and there are also reports of people becoming
disturbed, and others leaving because they became constantly sensitive to other people's bad vibrations. Needleman attributes the less successful experiences to a conflict
between mind and heart, one triumphing, and the other,
now submissive, open to Latihan forces or other forces not
attributable to divine energy. The helpers are instructed to
watch for emotional crises, and then terminate Latihan.
People who appear to be mad are said to be affected by "the
anger of God," according to Bapak, which results from
impatience and the intrusion of the heart or intellect into
the natural development. Bapak also warns against imagination preventing the return to the real essence.

Referring to women, Bapak warns against Latihan during menstruation. When a woman is giving birth, Latihan is taking place in her. He also suggests that the menstrual period is "really a Latihan," and advises rest for women during this time.

Although Latihan may have great permanent psychological benefits, there is another Subudian practice known as testing, with possibly more day-to-day value. It usually begins after the regular Latihan, and one can ask such questions as to whether one should marry a particular person, give up drugs, or take a job which has been offered. Then one permits Latihan to start again and awaits the inner feelings. The theory seems to be, to go beyond the mind arguing various alternatives and reach for a deeper intuition. One mother, despite her friends' advice, found that taking a job in the Park Service helped her teen-age son to discover himself. One can also ask the helper to test a problem of one's own.

Bapak, despite his statement against teaching, does have opinions on sex, the army, and death. Before intercourse he suggests calm, and advises against sex after the couple has been arguing, even with others. Children may be affected by the psychological state of the parents at the time of conception; it has been said that Subud children are "unusually kind and gentle." The Eastern approach on sex may be deeper than Freud's, putting it in perspective rather than emphasizing it as Freud did.

Bapak advises continuance of ordinary life. He is in favor of an orderly society. On the draft—like Nichiren Shoshu—he maintains that it is inconsistent to obey some laws and not others. This argument is an area in which the Christian religions appear to be more progressive; some avant-garde Christians espouse a revolutionary non-violent philosophy on war. I sometimes suspect that most of the Eastern religions are motivated more by a desire to consolidate their foothold within America than risk alienating it by opposing the draft. Bapak supports a responsible commitment to the community, such as helping others.

The key to Subud is probably in its attitude toward death. Bapak considers the soul the source of life, and the heart, mind, and feelings later additions. Latihan, by relaxing these accretions, allows the soul to grow. The soul cannot grow when restricted by worldly thoughts. A narrow soul, according to Bapak, is devilish, and when the man dies, the soul is trapped by its confines. Latihan, by permitting the soul to expand, is a preparation for death. He warns that death can happen at any time, even under violent circumstances. So, correspondingly, Latihan should enable people to feel God's power under varying circumstances. Then death can strike at any time. Needleman observes that, according to Bapak, this "inner feeling" (i.e. Latihan), by means of which a man sees the ordinary self, "is precisely that which survives the death of the self."

Bapak is quoted as saying that Subud is not a teaching and that man can only seek God by surrendering himself entirely and not depending on his intellect, heart, or desires.

Though not specifically Eastern, Subud takes its name from an amalgam of the Sanskrit words, *Susila, Buddhi* and *Dharma* (the close similarity between "Subuh" in Bapak's name "Muhammad Subuh" and "Subud," the name of the religion, is apparently a coincidence). According to the pamphlet from the Carmel Valley Center, these words mean, "right living in accordance with the will of God," "the divine force within every creature including man," and "the attitude of trust, sincerity and submission toward God." The first and third seem indistinguishable. Brevity is not the soul of Eastern religions.

Bapak was born in 1901. Other Indonesian seers remarked on his powers, but not until 1925 did he have a revelation in which a light brighter than the sun, shaped as a spheroid, entered his head. For a while he tried to avoid this. He used to go to movies (and still does). Prior to his religious vocation he was a local government employee on Java, an island of Indonesia. Bapak retired and turned to transmitting Subud. For a quarter century it spread slowly in Indonesia. In the 1950s some Westerners were attracted to Subud. In 1957 it spread to Europe and America.

Bapak does not want publicity and is married with children. Though Bapak, like the Pope, travels from one center to another he has appointed the helpers to initiate new people. Although Bapak is in a constant state of Latihan, his followers are not and are encouraged to lead normal lives.

CHAPTER V

Scientology

As organized as the Hare Krishna movement, but much larger, is Scientology, with "five million followers" in the U. S. I estimate six hundred thousand followers. It's all based on the teachings of L. Ron Hubbard, an American non-fiction writer, who is commodore of the "Sea Org," the administrative organization that floats around the world on nine ships. From his photograph on the jacket cover of his book, *The Fundamentals of Thought,* Hubbard looks like a friendly, strong-jawed, successful man in his late sixties. The Church of Scientology also describes his previous occupations as "explorer, travel writer, Lt., U. S. Naval Reserve commanding escort vessels during WWII, and screen writer. (Reference: 'Who's Who in the South and Southwest.')" From his yacht he conducts research into the higher realms of Scientology and archeology. Scientology with its emphasis on increasing one's ability and improving one's relations with others, reminded me in some ways of the Coué movement of the Teens and Twenties—"Day by day, in every way, I am getting better and better."

Thanks to Scientology, a great many people have been helped—or have helped themselves with its aid. An ex-Scientology disciple said, "Scientology is the religion of 'making it" in modern America." There is a parallel between a typical American dream of becoming the corporation president and owning a yacht and Hubbard's life today, but then the Pope lives in the Vatican and the Archbishop of Canterbury resides in Lambeth Palace.

Disciples relate unpleasant events in their past life to an auditor, a "pastoral counselor" or confessor, while gripping two tin cans attached to an "E" meter, an invention of L. Ron Hubbard's, consisting of a small electrically operated box with a dial. Similar to a lie detector it appears to be affected by how hard or how softly one grips the cans. The Scientologists say that once a person has "seen" a painful experience, he is free of it. A five-hour session costs $175. There are also communication courses: disciples sit facing each other in rows, learning how to look with ease at another person in front of him. The idea is to work one's way up through a series of grades of personality development until a person is "clear." Scientologists conduct a "holy war" (See *The Nation,* September 29, 1969, and *The Nation,* March 16, 1970, for a Scientology letter of rebuttal.) against psychiatrists—unbalanced, except for their justifiable attacks on mental imprisonment, shock treatment, brain surgery, and the abuse of powerful drugs.

There was lots of enthusiasm and vitality in the gathering in the ornate, gilt reception room of L. Ron Hubbard's New York center, which occupies a floor of the Hotel Martinique. A pretty, light-haired girl, whom I shall call Kim Brennan, twenty, married, said Scientology had helped her to see her parents as individuals rather than as stereotypes. Brimming with confidence and zest, she felt she had become a much more alive, capable person. Her husband, John, twenty-two, now a minister in Scientology, once a musician in a rock-and-roll band, and a former student at Brooklyn College of Music, had discovered he could see realistically his failed romances. An attractive young couple, they liked the absence of rituals and were dedicated to their new religion.

In the publicity office of New York Scientology was a bulletin board applying to the damned and the saved among the press, with whom relations have been somewhat strained on occasions. *Persona non grata* were the *Phila-delphia Inquirer,* and ABC-TV among others. On *Persona grata* were two reporters from the *New York Daily News,* a *New Yorker* woman, NBC-radio and various others.

I was asked a number of questions about my personal religious beliefs, whether I had undergone psychiatry, and my attitudes toward Scientology in particular, Hare Krishna, Gurdjieff, and the Manson-type satanic cults.

"There have been numerous charges of excessive fees charged by Scientology," I said.

"L. Ron Hubbard said recently that he wished the church could be free and that we existed in a barter system. Unfortunately we do not," said the Reverend Michael McGee, a tall blue-eyed man of about thirty, wearing a dark three-piece suit. He had slight traces of an English accent. "I'm from Missouri," he said, "but I've lived in Canada . . . I had about four hours sleep last night. Scientology is worth it."

Sunja Ackerman, the pretty, pregnant, dark-haired P. R. assistant, said, "I was in debt and without a job. I spent fifteen dollars on a communications course. In three months I was out of debt and had made fifteen hundred dollars."

"What happens if someone signs up for, say, a one thou-sand dollar intensive course and then after a few sessions wants to quit? Will he get his money back?"

"Yes," said Reverend McGee, Assistant Guardian of the Church in New York. "We will ask him to sign a statement saying he is expelled and renouncing all further benefits. If he rejoins, he'll have to make an act of contrition."

The E-meter, I suggested, works either by increased sweat from tension or increased hand-pressure.

"No," said McGee, speaking as a true believer, standing at his desk, "There is a wheatstone bridge and when the two hands hold the tin cans the body forms a bridge with the current. Subconscious images and tensions cause a mass in the mind which increases the body's electricity."

"Scientology is drawn from the Hinayana teachings of Buddhism," said McGee.

"The difference between psychiatry and Scientology is illustrated by the following story: If a little boy in school says apples are blue instead of red, the Scientologists hope that when he grows up he will become a scientist and cross-breed red apples and plums and produce blue apples. The teacher will then have to say, 'I'm sorry, Johnny.' The psychiatrists will call little Johnny a schizophrenic and lock him up in a mental hospital."

The Reverend McGee, a lock of dark curly hair falling across his handsome face, persuaded me to press my palm against his. "Resist," he said. We both pushed. "Antagonism," he explained. "Now we will cooperate. You will go where my hand goes and I will go where yours does." By what struck me as an uncanny osmosis our two hands moved around together in little glides and rises, though I resisted the impulse to sweep his hand rapidly in one direction.

"A person is like this penny you moved around freely on the desk." He then covered the new coin with a desk file, a typewriter, the telephone, and some papers. "The individual cannot see," he said. "When he has a painful experience, he joins it, it stays with him." He covered his face with his fingers, and peered at me. Suddenly he removed his hand. "With Scientology he is clear."

The communication course cost fifteen dollars. There were four beginning Scientologists—a pretty dyed-blonde with prominent front teeth, fleshy square face, who looked like a secretary in a typing pool on Wall Street; a curly-haired boy with glasses and a sheepish grin; a casually-dressed broad-faced young man, unshaven, with a well-built body; and a rather tight-looking prissy youngster in a cheap blue suit, wearing neat sideburns. Their instructor was a dapperly-dressed young black, quite handsome.

They were led through complex explanations of "TR"'s, meaning "Training Routine," in stages and "ARC," which is "Affinity," "Reality," and "Communication." Three understood quickly.

"What does 'sundering' mean?"

"I don't know, man," said the well-built boy, with a grin. "But I can guess from the other words."

"Look it up in the dictionary," said the black.

The process was repeated with three more words, including "overwhelming," to the boredom of the others.

Sexy, pregnant, dark-haired Sunja said to me, "This boy has had a problem since childhood about thinking he was stupid."

We then faced each other in pairs. "Don't fidget, smile, giggle, or look somewhere else. Look in the eye of your partner. Communicate. You will do it for as long as you can," said the teacher.

The "stupid" boy smiled, grinned, and fidgeted. Then he calmed.

"You lose," said Sunja to me. "You looked at them."

"You lose," said Sunja. "Don't look down."

I stared into Sunja's eyes. She was an attractive woman. Would I go mad? I tried counting. She blinked once in two minutes. After about ten minutes the flesh of her face looked heavy as if in sleep, though her eyes were wide. After fifteen minutes she and I stopped. "I feel as if I'm coming out of the depths," I said.

"That's typical," she replied.

The four were still motionless.

Next stage was TR-3.

A dark-haired girl, moderately pretty, plumpish, with a gap between her two front teeth, said to the man opposite her, "Do birds fly?"

"No."

"Do birds fly?"

"Who's your hairdresser?"

"This is TR-3. This is communication. I want you to answer my question. Do birds fly?"

"Yes."

"Thank you. Do birds fly?"

"You have a funny face."

"Do birds fly?"

"They work together," said Sunja, who had green-white-brown eyes, as I well remembered from looking at them for fifteen minutes. "He will harass her in a friendly way. She will try to get him to communicate. Then they'll switch around."

TEXAS

Frank Sargeant, president of Scientology, Austin, sat in the office located above a beauty salon and a real estate office. L. Ron Hubbard's literature was neatly deployed on shelves.

"People used to say, 'You'll be like a machine. When you get to be clear, you won't have any emotions left.' It isn't true, as you have lots of emotions when you're clear. . . .

"Relations with the people in Austin have been fine. We're on the Council of Churches. . . . A fellow in a 7-11 store said to me, 'You ought to read this. It would do you good.' . . . He wasn't a friend then, he is now [It was a Scientology book]. . . .

"We have more older people here than at most Scientology centers . . .

"Yes. That's the daughter of one of our auditors."

"Do you have youngsters, too?" I asked. (She was pushing a toy train on the dark-green carpeted floor)

". . . That's a lady who's come up from Corpus Christi [two hundred miles away] for a week to take a course. . . . Most of our people are training to be auditors so they can audit others. . . . One student will audit another."

"Is the emphasis on training auditors to expedite expansion of Scientology in the Austin area?"

"Yes. At 2 P.M. on Sunday we have from twenty to seventy present at our service. . . . We have confession and baptism. . . . We have about thirty-eight taking our auditing course right now. . . . It costs five hundred dollars." Sargeant was of medium height, an accountant, wearing a white buttondown shirt and brown suit. "The Christians say man has a soul, but that doesn't say what a man is," he said, smiling a little, "but Scientology says man is spirit and has a mind and a body."

PHOENIX

The Scientology center in Phoenix—within sight of the mountain ranges—is the size of a small medical clinic. Several times an old man with a tanned face and a pot belly crept past on his one good leg, the other one rigid. Later a woman of about thirty greeted the head of the center, "I feel so happy."

Here in Phoenix, in the years 1950 to 1954, is where Scientology began; where L. Ron Hubbard lived at the time. "But it died out after he left," said Henry Schlichting, about fifty-five years old, the chief Scientologist. "I came here in 1964, started it up and now there are two thousand members who support this center. Before processing I was accident-prone and suffered from a whiplash car injury to my neck which led to arthritis. Once it began, I stopped. I was a naturopathic physician, like an osteopath." He was a tall avuncular man—tanned like everyone else in Phoenix. Mr. Schlichting was an O.T.-6. The aim of Scientology is to reach "Clear." That is when one is cleared of all past "engrams" or problems. Beyond "Clear" are stages of spiritual development known as "Operating Thetan's," rising from "OT-1" to the highest "OT-6," though Hubbard is said to be working on "OT-7" and "OT-8."

LOS ANGELES

Scientology is giving employment to considerable numbers of auditors, ministers, and administrators. Like the growth of monasteries in Spain during the sixteenth and seventeenth centuries, these people are essentially non-productive in terms of the staples of life. Not too far from their downtown Los Angeles headquarters, at 2005 Ninth Street, which is the national headquarters, are two Spanish-style buildings, slightly rundown, in an equally drab area. One is the basic processing building and behind it is a two-story structure of offices for the national office. Around the corner in a smaller one is the "Advanced Organization" for

Clear and O.T. development. There are courses for training in general practical knowledge and to audit; but to go clear you also have to audit.

During the afternoon I saw perhaps fifty men and women, mainly young, working there, as well as the usual large number of students, many of them the inevitable hip and body-conscious actors and actresses.

L. Ron Hubbard's office was immaculate; it had a white chair with a white ribbon carefully placed across the seat. He is never there, although part of his private office is used for auditing. In the "Advanced Org" building was another "holy" office.

Karl Martin, young and serious, said, "We have three boats in Los Angeles—a twenty-foot, a thirty- to forty-footer and also a one hundred and twenty-foot one in drydock."

SEATTLE

The woman on the other end of the phone said, "Come at 10 A.M." So I did, driving up to a group of offices on the waterfront of Seattle with the usual Dianetics-Scientology signs outside. On entering I was confronted by two middle aged ladies, both wearing fairly heavy makeup and with hair curled in the style of the 1950s.

One told me her name.

The other, round-faced, gazing at me with wide blue eyes, said, "I'll only give you this interview if you sign this sheet of paper. It's our May Fifth directive. I'm the assistant guardian responsible for 6000 parishioners. I'm not going to have another article like the Saturday Evening Post. . . . I want to be on top of the press. We don't need the press. I told the man from CBS to drop dead. It's my religion. How dare they have a psychiatrist on? What does he know about Scientology, giving us a lot of crap."

DETROIT

It was a mid-June Sunday, a hot afternoon, sunny, the smog a white blanket over the West Ten-Mile road. There it was, a new office building, two-stories high, whitewashed brick and tinted glass, and inside on the bulletin board "Detroit Scientology Institute 205 . . . 207." The building's white letters on the black entrance roof said: TOPPER OFFICE CENTER.

I read the very curious little book (it is only 128 pages), *Fundamentals of Thought* by L. Ron Hubbard.

"He wrote such good science fiction. If only he hadn't started up that crazy cult," lamented a Haverford student, grinning. He went on, "A girl at Bryn Mawr and her boyfriend at Haverford were pushing Scientology a lot and giving tests last year, but at the beginning of this year interest dropped off. They separated, so he left Scientology."

Hubbard's book contains much worthwhile wisdom and to a lesser extent some surprising statements. However (like the Bible which in Episcopalism and Roman Catholicism has been modified and has evolved in interpretation), some of its tenets have recently been abandoned, one Scientologist minister told me.

The *Fundamentals of Thought* reminds the reader of the H-bomb's potential threat to all life. It explains exactly who we are, where we came from, and where we are going. By following its advice we will succeed in this world, maximizing our talents. It promises immortality. And finally it says that Scientology is the truth, and there is none other. To a searcher it could be the answer, guaranteeing a fruitful life ahead. The Rev. Steven Beisher, Minister of Public Relations, writes, "Any curing of physical illnesses is conducted by a medical doctor. If a person is physically ill and desires Dianetic Pastoral Counseling, the Minister is required by Church policy to send the preClear to a medical doctor for treatment. It is part of the creed of the Church that 'the spirit alone can save or heal the body.' We do not treat or cure physical ills. But through professional medical attention addressed to the body and pastoral counseling addressed to the spirit, we do guarantee health and happiness as a final obtainable result."

Naturally the following statements have caused many

non-Scientological eyebrows to rise, and I have picked them at random, for there are many (if I may imitate the author's tone of certainty):

"No such knowledge has ever before existed and no such results have ever before been attainable by Man as those which can be reached by a study of this brief volume." From page one—this may be at least half-true, at least in regard to results, if Scientology's extraordinary growth is accepted.

On page 65 Hubbard says that a spirit (or "thetan" in Scientology terminology) can increase or decrease a body's weight. "This test has actually been made and an increase of as much as thirty pounds, actually measured on scales, has been added to and subtracted from a body by creating 'mental energy.' "

"Scientology processing among other things can improve the intelligence quotient of an individual, his ability or desire to communicate, his social attitudes, his capability and domestic harmony, his fertility, his artistic creativity, his reaction time and his health." Page 92.

There are several immediately noticeable strands in the fabric of this at times obscure work—its adoption or synthesis of mental health, its similarity to Platonism, its emphasis on achieving self-reliance and competing in a winning way.

The latter part of the book, dealing with auditing preClears, urges the student to detach from past traumas, tells the auditor to listen, directs him to intervene when the preClear speaks too long and becomes self-destructive, warns the auditor not to "evaluate for the preClear."

There are Hubbard's eight "Dynamics"—the urge toward existence as one's self; the urge toward self as a sexual or bisexual activity, including family and children; group existence; "The urge toward mankind"; toward "the animal kingdom"; toward "the physical universe"; toward spirits; and the eighth—God.

There are Hubbard's three laws—the spirit called a "thetan," the mind, and the body.

By self-awareness the thetan can control his mind and body. Thus this book is "All and Everything"—to borrow Gurdjieff's title.

A very important book of Scientology is *Dianetics,* first published in 1950, a best-seller even then, the success of which led to the development of today's organization. A relatively brief examination of this 445-page volume indicates it presents Hubbard's spiritual technique; as Reverend Beicher says, the preClear or thetan, is assisted by the Pastoral Counselor, to become himself in the present.

The absence of spiritism reveals an early stage of Scientology, later phases of which contain increasing emphasis on the supernatural.

Hubbard writes on page 400: "In twenty or a hundred years the therapeutic technique which is offered in this volume will appear to be obsolete."

On page 182: "For each man is a great deal different from every other man. His inherent personality is different."

In terms of tedium the author's prediction as to the obsolescence of *dianetics* appears to have been fulfilled.

One day after one of my encounters with Scientology I wrote that these seemed to me "people very on the ball, people very efficient, people always smiling in a forced way, people ludicrously nasty, people charming, chilling, suspicious, likable, touching, beautiful."

CHAPTER **VI**

Spiritual
Science

That there is an expansion of Spiritualism in the U. S. is
agreed on by all observers of the religious scene. *Newsweek*
of April 13, 1970, quotes the National Council of Churches
as estimating "at least one hundred and fifty thousand"
members in "over four hundred" spiritualist groups, although they do not give out membership figures. Once
popular in the 1920s, the old spiritualism emphasized
seances while the new often consists of mediums running
little "churches," accepting "fixed 'donations' " and "delivering messages from the spirits."

The problems in discussing Spiritualism are several. De-
fining it is an immediate difficulty, for it wanders into a
wide spectrum of magical activities. Even the word "magical" may be inaccurate, as some people would include Dr. J.
H. Rhine's investigations into parapsychology. There is a
connection with numerology, Tarot, mediums conversing
with the dead, astrology, Espiritismo which is followed by
some black and Spanish-speaking Americans, and satanic
groups. Another drawback to coherent presentation is the
suspicion and rigid independence of many Spiritualists
who refuse to acknowledge the existence of each other. It is
a field of rugged individualists operating in worlds of their
own to such an extent that often the other world is the only
safe place for them to express their personalities fully. A

Spiritualist in New York City whom I know, who was otherwise very cooperative, replied, when asked about other Spiritualists and churches, "I don't know. I have nothing to do with them. I can't help you."

One expert in this subject, who asked that his name not be printed out of fear of being pestered by phone calls and letters from neurotic Spiritualists, told me, "People are joining them [Spiritualist churches] in increasing numbers, but they are not considered by most people as bonafide religions. They are para-religions. It is a specialized activity attempting to communicate with spirits of the dead. Spiritualism has no teachings on the meaning of man's existence and how he should conduct himself [This, as will be seen later in this chapter, is probably an oversimplification]. It is a highly specialized form of psychology not related to the whole society."

Connecting Spiritualism with the efflorescence of Eastern beliefs in general, he remarked, "Eastern religions understand the self, develop self-control and security among a subculture, but they are not strong enough to influence overall patterns of our society unlike Christianity, which does."

The *Yearbook of American Churches,* published by the National Council of the Churches of Christ in the U.S.A., provides statistical information on two hundred and forty-seven American religious groups. However, it lists only two major Spiritualist organizations—the National Spiritual Alliance of the U.S.A., R.F.D., Keene, New Hampshire, and the National Spiritualist Association of Churches. The first one listed Mrs. Marion A. Pelletier as secretary and Mrs. Jeanette R. Brown of 16 Congress Place, Fitchburg, Massachusetts, as president. The second organization reported The Rev. Robert J. MacDonald as president at P.O. 147, Cassadoga, Florida. The yearbook was not supplied with any other data, and when I wrote these individuals, I received a reply only from the Reverend MacDonald, whom I shall quote later.

A review of Spiritualism might include the following

phenomena, besides those mentioned above: Do the activities of the late Bishop James Pike fall within the purlieu of Spiritualism? What about the Rev. Arthur Ford, a well-known Spiritualist? What about the clairvoyant Jeane Dixon, whose book, *A Gift of Prophecy,* has sold over three million copies? Edgar Cayce's Association for Research and Enlightenment (see Chapter XVI) deals with aspects of Spiritualism in the general sense. An examination of such a rich source as New York City's Eighth Street Bookshop shows a bewildering and numerous variety of books on reincarnation and tales from the dead and prophecies by a wide selection of people.

Newsweek says that Spiritualism, as distinct from Espiritismo, appeals to whites. It traces historically to Rosicrucianism and theosophy, which began in the nineteenth century, thanks to Madam Blavatsky. There was a craze in the 1920s for seances which featured table-rapping, but nowadays telling fortunes and being in touch with spirits for commercial purposes is illegal in many states. This apparently is why mediums are now more respectable, maintaining churches, asking only for donations.

It should be clear that Spiritualism as such is not new in the U.S. It should be clear that as a religion it has virtually no organization or shared beliefs. It is so vague that in a sense it covers everything and nothing, so I will not attempt to link a host of disparate people, many of whom would protest strongly at being included in the same chapter, or try for order where obviously there is none. I have instead concentrated on one Spiritualist, who may have little connection with any of the others, and yet who may, by being presented at some length, shed some light—as a single bird when studied gives much general information applicable to all ornithological species—on Spiritualism as a whole.

A minister in the Spiritual Science Mother Church, the Rev. Ellen Resch, a medium, has introduced her flock to her teacher, Winn, a being from another world, and to less important spirits. At her candlelit services three nights a week, Tuesday, Friday, and Saturday, in a room in New

York City's Steinway Hall, Ellen, a middle-aged, German-born woman dressed in white satin, goes into a trance and, with graceful fishlike motions, tells her one hundred and fifty disciples what Winn and the other assorted spirits say to her. Winn and the other spirit teachers—through Ellen—encourage each participant and warn them of dangers in the upcoming week. Also, Ellen, an attractive blonde, tells them in a lyric voice of their "Karma," the record of all the events in a person's past and future existence. Several of the congregation saw visions during one meditation period.

From the podium Ellen begins: "I guess I always have to be happy, otherwise you wouldn't be happy either [the young people laugh]." Everyone recites the Twenty-third Psalm. She then talks about "negative feelings over the Memorial Day holiday. Please, dear spirit, get me out of the dumps. You can read a good book or even watch a good television show. You can build up karmic debts, I'm sorry to say, from brooding but you can build up karmic credits. Almost all of you are going through change. You're not going to let it, as you say, frig you. You may not find instant bliss in this life, but perhaps in two, five, or ten lives." There followed a two-minute long silent meditation. Mrs. Resch, who talks to people "ten hours a day," popped a Luden's lozenge in her mouth. There was a collection, and the plate was filled with dollar bills. For the next hour Mrs. Resch went into a kind of trance. With her eyes closed, gesticulating energetically, she gave each young person practical advice and a message from their spirit-teacher combined with practical advice. "David, let your lantern shine brighter," she said to one. "Frank, you have expended much energy over the weekend. The name of your spirit teacher in Tibet is C-O-S-T-O-S."

One of the group was Mia Howard, nineteen, a hair-dresser, just married to an actor, "Hash," who had a minor role as a hippie in *Midnight Cowboy*. She has brown eyes, short well-groomed hair. She and Hash met at the Spiritual Science services. Mia said, "I went to the Catholic Church for years, but the nuns and priests are such hypocrites,

preaching love of God and your neighbor, and then they do
the opposite. They have negative vibrations. When I came
here and heard about the spirits like Winn's, Ellen's
Teacher, and Domper, the one assigned to me by Winn,
and Ruby, my guide, I knew I was no longer lonely. Winn
assigned Domper as my special teacher. Domper was my
teacher in an earlier life in Tibet when I was a boy there.
Ruby is the spirit of an American Indian. He is my guide, a
lower order of spirit than Domper, and may in the future
be reincarnated again as a human being. If down in the
dumps, I can hear in my head Domper say 'Mia' sharply,
and Ruby will sometimes call my name in fun. Tonight,
through Ellen, Winn said a number of pieces of paper were
coming together in my life, which I interpreted as the hair-
pieces I put together in my work."

Hash said, "I said, 'Hello, Hi,' to Ellen over the phone
and she drew a soul chart in pastel colors with a one-hun-
dred-word explanation underneath and it was fantastically
accurate.

"Now my spirit teacher is Hale, who is from Tibet, and
my guide is White Feather, an American Indian. The guide
is a lower species of spirit who has not developed out of
what the Indian philosophers call the Wheel of Incarnation. He may yet come back for another life, though not
while I am alive. Hale is a free spirit.

"Coming to Ellen has brought me peace and love and
patience. For the first year I had private consultations—
about seven. It was strange but from the beginning I knew
it was right. Previously I had been on thirty-seven LSD
trips and two methedrine."

He and Mia had just been married by Ellen.

Donnie, twenty-one, who had a lead role in a one-day-
long Broadway show, said, "There's a lot of similarity between Ellen and a psychoanalyst. I went to a psychoanalyst
for six months, but he did not scratch the surface. I was a
Presbyterian, and confirmed, but it was boring, though I
believe in Jesus."

They all said, as we sat in a drugstore booth after the service, "Ellen shows you can become part of God."

Mrs. Resch gave me a one-page report on a woman-seeker's "soul pattern painting." Done by Ellen in July, 1969, she wrote that the person's emanation was lively and strong. She said she had faith and self-certainty, the latter quality portrayed by the color blue. Orange demonstrated instinctual ability. She deeply understood the spirit, which was indicated by purple for prayer and white for meditation. The woman was in touch with the mind of God, was "emotionally sensitive [light green], you give a lot of energy, [red] to others, perhaps too much sometimes [darker green]." In an important earlier life, the woman had been a sculptress and painter in Greece. Finally Ellen predicted that the woman would make progress, suffering less from "stress and strain." She would become stronger. There would be some unexpected visitors who would bring happiness, particularly in September and October. Ellen concluded, "Look forward to this time with special anticipation. Love to you."

Mrs. Resch granted me an interview in the hotel where she lived. It's a drab, gaudy place, but her two rooms were colorfully (lots of reds and oranges) and tastefully decorated. There were a number of oriental bead necklaces and a sort of tiny altar. There she received persons wanting private advice.

"Spiritual science believes in the universal spirit, the teachings of the Scriptures [Christian, Indian, Buddhist], reincarnation and love between neighbors. There are no dogmas," she said in her dulcet cheerful tones. "The Christian Churches have become too rule conscious."

About a year and a half ago young people suddenly started to come to her studio, eventually driving her older followers away. One reason was a "soul chart" she did for a young woman writer and her roommate. Principally, she said, it was because of the Aquarian Age and the astrological influence of Neptune which causes greater probing into

the spirit. Many old spirits came back into the young
people who come to her (see the chapter on Edgar Cayce).

She emphasized a balance between "humility and self-con-
fidence, avoidance of the power game. When a young actor
says to me, 'I want to be a famous actor,' I say, 'Do you want
to be famous or do you want to be an actor?' "

She said she worked twelve hours a day, seven days a
week. German born, she has been in this country for some
time and was married to a painter who died two years ago.
She had been an astrologer. "We are going out into space
and deeper into the mind," she commented. Ellen, though
always charming, was secretive about her past, saying that
mediums did not like to talk about it.

The Reverend Macdonald sent me a recent copy of *The
Summit,* the official church publication of the National
Spiritualist Association of Churches, along with a note saying that the secretary "will send you such material as he
may feel will be helpful to you." On the cover was an eerie
photograph of dark tree tops and a sunset sky with the sun
sending spooky rays against massive clouds. The magazine
itself described it as "Christmas Light in a darkening sky."
The lead article was about the 78th Annual Convention
held in Houston, which was evidently a success. Among
other events there was a friendship hour which started off
the meetings on the right foot. In some ways it sounded like
a nice, folksy Midwestern get-together. For example, they
went on a tour of the Astrodome. That first afternoon after
they had "partaken" of a light snack of coffee, tea, sandwiches and cakes, they all sang old-fashioned songs and
hymns. On Sunday they heard a speech on "Spiritualism—a
Spiritual Planet for The Space Age." However, the magazine did not explain what this was. After the speech there
was some clairvoyance by Trustees Ernst A. Schoenfeld and
Walter Holder. In his report the editor commented that
there were more representatives attending from more states
than there had been in many years. Switching from one
form of space to another, the spiritualists listened to a

speech by Dr. W. R. Downs of the NASA Space Center, talking about Apollo Eleven.

There was a service for those ministers and mediums, "who have made their transition into the other expression of life."

During a conference on teaching it was pointed out that the students as well as the teacher had to penetrate the "seemingly thick curtain" which kept apart the dead and the living. Life was not divided "into locked compartments" —students should look on life as continuously flowing. There was progress and change and no beginning nor ending.

In a conference on ministry they talked about a book which related a true story of an event in a seance. The medium's guide, called "Red Cloud," had transmitted a message from a young girl to the medium, asking the latter to get in touch with her mother. Apparently the girl had died on an Easter Monday, and nine years later the woman's son had been killed. The mother had been terribly upset and emotionally disturbed and knew nothing of the medium and her seance until the Spiritualist contacted her in another town. The mother was overjoyed. The story ended by mentioning that the mother herself "graduated to the Summerland [presumably heaven]," and subsequently gave thanks to the guide, Red Cloud, and through Red Cloud to the medium and hence on to the author of the book.

At another point in the magazine, four young correspondents noted the increase in the number of youths interested in Spiritualism. Evidently many were writing term papers, which showed a more open-minded viewpoint on the part of teachers.

A girl who attended another Spiritualist church in New York City struck me as follows: She wore Indian moccasins, orange trousers, orange and white top, had reddish long hair, a rough complexion over a face reminiscent of a horse. She had strange green eyes and, if saying something she thought I didn't like, would turn her head sideways and giggle. After the interview she made a sketch of my shadow. She gave me the feeling she was way out in a void—somewhere in an empty sphere. Once or twice I was afraid she was casting psychic spells—unpleasant ESP transmissions were being directed toward me.

CHAPTER VII

Religious Communes

GENERAL STORE, ARIZONA

Like Man, it was the usual hippie scene, or maybe that's an unkind word for them. They were initially suspicious, as expected, and then quite friendly and talkative, as half-expected.

Occasionally the two-way radio blared forth, connecting the general store and hippies or communies or just plain young people out there in the hills of Arizona, and the old sun was shining down, and the hills were dark green and this young person, male, with misshapen front teeth and glasses, in the traditional blue jeans, said:

"You ought to write about the new new religions."

He smiled shyly, showing his teeth. "Like in the Aquarian age, we're in Phase One. We're in Gestalt Therapy. We're on the verge of something new. We experience the miraculous. Just coming into a room and being part of it, aware of all of it and myself. Or washing dishes. That's miraculous. I put all of myself into it. I used to find it a drag for fifty people."

"You're hired," said a chick.

An attractive girl of about eighteen, wearing an almost see-through loose blouse and barely visible blue-jean shorts, came in and whispered in his ear.

52

He smiled. "That's bad. Someone's got the clap. We all had it. Then we took a thirty-day abstinence, but I guess this chick came and was here for a few days."

Another girl with long reddish brown hair said, "Some of them in the communes are into the native American religions . . . peyote . . . but they're secretive about it . . . The Hopis have those Kivas." She went into a long story about the destruction of the earth three times, the similarity to the Biblical flood, hiding in ant holes, and the expectation of the destruction of the entire world.

At the general store were supplies of all kinds of macrobiotic foods—wheat and honey. A sign said the winter had been "bad" and the communes could not feed any more newcomers. Beside books on Zen macro-biotics there was one on Edgar Cayce, and health food, and another by Teilhard de Chardin.

The funny-toothed boy said, "My commune's 'The Family.' One of us was half-paralyzed on one side—with palsy—and we all put our hands on his head and two days later he was completely recovered."

"The information center does a better job as a police force than the local police," said a somber young man who worked at an information center adjacent to the store and a clinic all run by and for the hippies. The town was quite alive to Chicanos beating up hippies. The local paper was running stories on local government attempts to close the communes down on the grounds of being a health risk, and the artistic community, which was there long before the hippies, was protesting about "fascist" police repression.

A magazine, *The Modern Utopian,* (which was on sale in the general store) published quarterly at 2441 LeConte, Berkeley, California, contains an article, "The Mystical Experience and the Mystical Commune," subtitled "Eighteen hip religious communes and the beliefs of the people who inhabit them," by Stanley Krippner, Ph. D., Director, Dream Laboratory, Maimonides Medical Center, Brooklyn, New York, and Don Fersh, a student at the University of

New Mexico and research aide at Maimonides. The article starts: "Communal living, an ingrained heritage in the United States since the Transcendental Movement of the 1820s, is undergoing a dramatic revival." It says present-day communes are as "numerous and diverse as . . . those of the Fourierists, Shakers, Moravians, Zoarites, Perfectionalists, and Spiritualists [Carden, 1969]." It points to the existence "for decades" of the "Amish and Mennonite communities." Besides studying secular communes, which are both "relatively unstructured" and "relatively structured," the authors visited among the eighteen communes "the structured, highly-organized religious commune."

Krippner and Fersh "spent time" in "California's Now House" and New York's "Avenanda Ashram." At the "Road #721" commune they reported: "The natural setting of the commune fosters a type of pantheism in which God is found in all forms of life; as a result, paranormal communications—with animals and birds as well as with humans—is taken for granted." At Libre commune "the *I Ching* is often consulted by both adults and children." At the Placitas (New Mexico) commune, the leader, Ulysses S. Grant, is "purportedly a reincarnation of the General." In New Mexico the Morning Star East commune "adheres to a religious outlook which can be dubbed 'mystical Christianity.'"

The Modern Utopian described a life-style, now almost certainly over, at the "Chosen Family" commune in California where the founder is in "Marin State Hospital suffering from . . . a physical breakdown," where there were "two large scale drug raids," where "a visitor was killed riding a motorcycle around Novato," where "a ranch horse" wandered onto "Highway 101 killing itself and a motorist," where "the mansion" was gutted by fire, where "two little girls" died after falling "into the unfenced swimming pool." A photograph shows "family members," while the girls were in the intensive care ward of the hospital, chanting "a Hindu prayer" for them.

UR COMMUNE

The Ur Commune, a new group in the mountains of Wyoming, has published the following report:

It is about a new type of greenhouse they say they have invented. The altitude of the mountainside where the experiment was done is about five thousand feet. The temperature variations are extreme, ranging to a low of minus thirty degrees Fahrenheit on winter nights. The season for growing vegetables is from ninety to a hundred days long.

A tiny section of the mountainside is cut out of the S/SW facing slope (ground does not freeze five feet down—maximum depth is eight feet) the S/SW orientation captures the winter sun. Auxiliary heat comes from a green manure pile (one hundred ten to one hundred twenty degrees Fahrenheit) in a large box in the back. They say that two of the men aided in obtaining the supplies, 1016 vinyl-two-skins with air-cap-bubble plastic sandwich. By early March shoots were coming up.

The report hopes that this successful scheme will help to eliminate pollution from fuels such as oil and coal, that it will replace chemically-treated foods and will result in similar vegetable structures being built all over the West to help combat poverty. They call their device a "food house," but it is widely known in horticulture as the winter-heated pit.

In the office of Laramie's "Spring is Alive" school, (the name deriving from an Indian word) a free private place for children from nursery age up to twelve, I met Frank, who was a teacher there, an admirer of Gurdjieff, and the only member of the Ur Commune to work outside of it.

Frank introduced me to Betsy Wilson, a long-haired brunette with hair streaked by the sun and brown eyes half-hidden by eyelids. We drove to Ur—over dirt-rutted roads. Miles away across the valley against the green forested mountainside was a tiny yellowish dome.

"I've been married three times, I'm thirty-three." With
her was her son, Fred, a six-year-old with blond hair and a
silent, sometimes pouting face. "My first husband was
thirty-five. My family wanted me to marry him. He came
from quite a comfortable background. After he carried me
across the threshold he spoke not more than five words to
me for the next two months. He was a homosexual. Twenty-
three days after my divorce I remarried. My second husband
beat me up every day and threatened to kill me three times,
but I guess he was more real than my first one for the marriage lasted seven months. I lived with my third husband for
two years before marrying him . . . an ex-convict, he could
not get work. Fred was born. I was supporting him and my
husband with help from my family and paying his ex-wife's
alimony, too. After a year and seven months I split. That
was five years ago." She answered my questions easily.
There was a kind of light air about her, in the sense that
her character or soul or personality—call it what you will—
seemed to be floating above ground.

Suddenly at the top of the sunbaked trail was a large
dome with wings and another one a hundred yards up the
mountainside without extensions. There were glass windows in the eight-sided roofs. They looked across a vast
valley, tinted light blue and white and beige, to a rolling
mountain range. The sun was still high in the blue western
sky. The elevation was five thousand feet.

There were several hippie-looking men and women
working at various jobs in the clearing among the pines. A
few children were dancing and running or walking. There
was a vegetable field. A goat was being milked by a black-
haired man and a very pretty red-haired girl. Set in among
the trees were some A-frame dwellings.

Betsy said, "I spent two months here two summers ago.
This time—a month. Five of us single ones—Peter, Jane,
John, Bob, and I—live in this A-frame," a pleasant disor-
dered dwelling. "We dress and undress in front of each
other. I've never had sex here. You don't need it. We are
celibate. I've never masturbated." She laughed. "Last year
in the Ashram, Max [one of the new members of Ur] and

Dorothy [the wife of Len] fell in love, but everyone was sensible about it. I haven't had sex in a year up until a month ago, and I think I'm going to return to celibacy."

In the library of the big cantilevered building a young woman was illustrating a manuscript by Swami Ananda who was Lawrence Edgar, a famous ex-political radical. Edgar is a friend of James Henderson's, the strongest personality at Ur. Edgar had studied under a Guru in India and had just finished teaching at Ur, leaving his book to be completed by other members in intricate Eastern illustrations. The sheets were lying on the worktable, the vast pages covered with multitudinous hands and arms and eyes and sometimes drawings of commune members at work. Nearby were shelves with books on Subud, Gurdjieff-Ouspensky's *The Fourth Way*, Christ, Buddha, the Essenes, Judaism, and Vedanta. This group seemed to be worshipping everyone.

On the second level of the dining-room-kitchen, we sat together on cushions, our sandals and sneakers on the ladder-steps outside, the early evening sun coming in through the windows.

We chanted an Eastern mantra for almost ten minutes. We then linked hands for a minute's silent meditation.

That same slightly sickening smell I had suffered from in a New York religious center—of decaying fruit. Unwashed hands. A small child to my left dropped yogurt on me. An edible main course of macaroni, cheese and cauliflower, a fruit salad, a revolting sage tea served with honey (the next day I was mildly ill).

"Sage is native," said one of the nineteen adults and children sitting around the octagonal table, open in the center to serve as walk area for the server and also as an opening to the kitchen below. On the wall there was a scroll, a sort of hymn to God.

"We get twenty-five to thirty-two eggs daily from our thirty-eight chickens."

"A farmer in town gets thirty-two from thirty-three daily."

"Yes with amphetamines and twenty-four hour lights."

Every voice could be heard distinctly across the twenty-foot diameter, but the acoustics were soft. (There seemed to be an unusually large number of blue eyes among those present.)

After dinner in the other oblong building in the great meeting hall with a huge window to the east, sitting on the edges of its six-foot diameter was a man whose black hair was shaved almost to the skin. He looked like a guru and had a birdlike face. Beside him was the very pretty red-head.

How to apply the spiritual life to being a New York City landlord was the subject of our discussion: "You cannot maintain buildings under rent control. I own buildings in Brooklyn. With some tenants paying less than twenty dollars a room and old ladies getting eighty-five dollars a month social security, you support them. I live in a commune."

"Which one?"

"Brooklyn . . . forty thousand people there are my friends. I know them all." His name was Ralph Ford, and he had been away from New York for almost a year in Central America. He and his girl friend were spending two weeks here.

Ralph said, "The twentieth century has gone wrong. No one likes it, not even Richard Nixon. We export our materialistic society to other countries and they imitate it. Society went off the tracks in the Industrial Revolution. There were wars in the medieval ages but within the community or the feudal state you were protected, and people liked each other."

That night there was to be "a discussion of plans" at the meeting in the "Soul" room, and I assumed I would not be allowed to attend.

"My principal objection," said John, "is that you should spend a month here instead of a day. You won't know anything more at the end of the meeting. Ur is inside, not outside."

Said James, "All you writers, I think, go part way into

ways of living such as ours but you never commit your-
selves."

"Granted," I said, "But I can learn something. I have
stayed in monasteries at times during the past years. I even
considered joining one, but their life was not for me. Perhaps I should join you, but I don't have time. I have to
research religions all over the country and have the book to
the publishers on a deadline. That's the way it is."

They decided I would be allowed to attend. Three bells
hanging from a cord suspended between posts were struck
by a youngish man swinging an eight-foot log. The bells
were in odd shapes, one looked like a kerosene stove, but
they rang as sonorously as those I had once heard in a
Benedictine monastery.

The "Soul" room was an adobe house used for daily
meditation at six-thirty in the morning and eight-thirty in
the evening. The interior was dark and slightly smoky from
a fire at the end opposite the three-foot-high entrance
through which the others and I crawled through to enter.
There was the smell of incense.

"We always walk clockwise in the 'Soul' room," said
Betsy.

Someone whispered, "Take off your shoes."

There was a square pit with a candle and several bowls of
wheat kernels. Surrounding the pit were two tiers where
the Ur-lovers sat on comfortable cushions and rugs. There
were shawls around most of the women and several of the
men and women were in the half-Lotus position. A tiny
gong was sounded. There was silence for a long while.

A voice said, "Oh God, enlighten us and bring the truth
to our lips."

The following dialogue occurred over the next forty-five
minutes which in very condensed treatment may be best
presented in a diagrammatic step form, for this was almost
the way it happened. The conversation or service was almost clockwise, which was the chronological way it happened—accidentally (or perhaps in a mystical Eastern way
not so fortuitously). Start with James Henderson, a stout

handsome man, at the top of the drawing. The conversations, as they occurred are numbered in sequence:

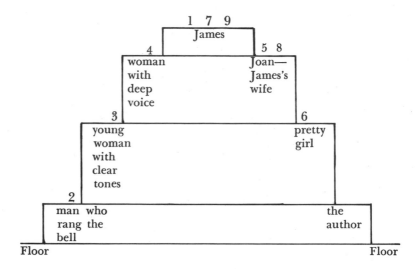

1. *James*: We have been living in the daisy field. Tonight I would like to suggest three changes to deepen our spiritual life for the next ten days: One, we substitute Ur for all names and pronouns. Two, we eliminate the verb *to be* and three, we commit ourselves to God for twenty-four hours. For example, Countess Rowena would cease to exist and become Ur . . . .

2. *The voice of the man who rang the bell*: We have been in the daisy field, but we should try it.

3. *A young woman with clear tones*: Eliminating the verb *to be* is too difficult.

4. *Another deeper woman's voice*: Suggest three days instead of ten.

5. *Joan—James's wife*: How do we communicate with the children? James, would you be frustrated if we did not do this?

6. *A lilting pretty female voice*: I want to be part of God.

7. *James*: To become God is the objective.
8. *Joan*: I recommend we vote for points one and three.
9. *James*: I will accept the whole package or nothing.

Someone said, "The film company coming two days from now may have difficulty with their soundtrack." Laughter.

Everyone voted "Yes" (it had to be unanimous to pass) until it came to the turn of the girl with the pretty lilting voice. Someone said to her, "Dare you to vote 'No'" but she consented.

At the end we chanted "Ur—Ur—Ur—Ur" it happening naturally and not synchronously and yet the rhythm uniting as voices chimed in at various intervals. The stocky man beside me on the rug on the Adobe mud combined his "Ur"s with a musical yawn.

In the kitchen afterward I said to James, "Ur thanks Ur."

Two days later on a bright sunny morning John said, "James's domination of that meeting was coincidental and somewhat atypical. I don't feel like making a confrontation. After all I left personality conflicts behind . . . I do sometimes resent how newcomers usually seek James out for decisions."

"The two main buildings are made of sandstone," John and Frank said, "In time it will fall back into the earth. An Indian advised us on building and ranching problems. Edward Cooney helped with digging out the sandstone, we will help him construct a house this summer in return."

What I have, perhaps, omitted here is the sense of oneness with the community (at dinner especially), frequent feelings on that beautiful high location of being able to go out into nature and the whole world and the universe simultaneously coming into me. In the "Soul" room the oneness in the dark had more depth for me, and afterward, when we emerged, though no one said much of anything, I felt they were a part of me and me a part of them.

Ur is probably going somewhere, its members are slightly older than the usual religious commune.

That summer the hippies were coming into the vicinity of the town in the Rocky Mountains.

David Johnson, age nineteen, had a scooped nose, long hair fastened behind his ears with hairpins, handsome green eyes, broad chin, a tall body, and he looked and acted much like a saint—often smiling, usually relaxed, bobbing up and down with enthusiasm as he sat cross-legged on the couch in the hippie house which he owned. On his chest hung a small upside-down hand with a configuration in the palm, representing Buddha's left hand holding a third eye, and around his neck was an American Indian necklace. The house was on Desert Road—a drab area of weeds and tumbled down clapboard buildings.

"I went to a conventional prep school and to a state university for a while.

"I was in Baba, and stayed for two weeks at one of their Pacific Coast centers and then went to a house of Baba lovers in southern California.

"My parents traced me through the Baba center, as they knew the address of the place. Suddenly my father was standing outside. I was off drugs completely as one is when in Baba, but my parents were hysterical. My father tricked me. He said 'Come back to Cleveland for the weekend. I'll give you a plane ticket back.'

"At Cleveland Airport he drove straight to the mental hospital. I recognized it as I'd been going to a psychiatrist there about a year earlier. He used to mediate between my family and me, and he'd said, 'If you ever want a bed here for the night, let me know.' I guess I'd mentioned this in the past to my family, so my father remembered and said 'We have a full house for the weekend. And we thought our guests would bother you.'

"In the reception area they were filling out all these forms. I said, 'This is crazy, what's the point of this?' I said to my father, 'Look, put me up in the Holiday Inn, and I promise I won't see any of my friends.' This nurse was already standing there waiting for me. The doctor on duty was saying, 'This patient is showing panic symptoms,' and I *was* starting to get a little panicky. Finally they called my doctor, Doctor Raskin, who told me over the phone to spend the night and he'd come the next day. I followed the nurse and the door clicked behind, and I said, 'Am I locked in?'

"The older nurses were tough. I was allowed freedom for a while, but they kept me away from all women. They have complete control over you—your mind, body, and sex life. They tell you, 'You're crazy. That's why you're here. It's a standard symptom of craziness not to know you're crazy.' They can break you. There are these intern psychiatrists, less than thirty-years-old, who are aggressive young punks with short hair versus the young people with long hair.

"My own psychiatrist double-crossed me. I had some freedom to go into town, and then my parents heard about it, and raised hell with him, refusing to pay him any more, and complained to his superiors, 'You've got incompetent personnel here,' and so he refused to fight for me.

"One of the student nurses used to escort me into town— that was the only way I could date her. We spent a few afternoons at a student nurse's apartment. Making love under such circumstances is schizophrenic, as they have this power over you, and the keys they carry have a big sexual symbolism for them.

"The ironic thing about the hospital was that I went back onto drugs at the hospital. The hospital was a farce. It had a fashionable reputation for straightening out hippies.

"One day when my mother came to see me, I said, 'What do you think would happen to me if I was free for the next three days?' She started to cry and said, 'Either of three things—one—you'd go to Greenwich Village [I wasn't interested in Greenwich Village, but that shows you where they were at] two—you'd be dead in an alley from an overdose or three—you'd be dead in an alley having been stabbed while being robbed for drugs.'

"I don't blame my parents though, what with all the fears they had and the Depression and bringing up children.

"I said to them, 'Look, instead of spending seventy dollars a day here, let me fly to San Juan or somewhere else in the Caribbean and I promise I won't move out of my hotel room.'

"I was moved to a hospital in Baltimore and that really was the clink. I was all alone with only me to say I wasn't crazy. I had to get out of there. Otherwise I might be there for life.

"So with friends I smuggled out my electric guitar. Then another friend took the guitar case containing my clothes and money I'd saved up secretly bit by bit and had hidden. Then one morning I was about to walk out of the ward to go to the music therapy building. I had three minutes because the ward always telephoned the music building to say I had left, and then an accomplice in the hospital phoned the music building to say my doctor, Jones, had stopped me for a conference. Another call went to the ward itself to say my doctor was seeing me for a while.

"Just as I was going out the door, one of the administrator doctors calls me harshly into his office, 'Johnson!' There was a mix-up over the previous day when I had missed lunch by practicing music with permission and he had not been told. I was scared because I had only three minutes to get to the car which was then going to leave as it was on the grounds and they had these patrol cars going around all the time.

"I walked out the door toward the music building and veered past the music building and got into the car.

"I then disappeared for a while as my family had the police and F.B.I. after me.

"My brother was one of the guys who helped, though he used to tell my parents all sorts of things about me, and there was no way I could disprove them. The next time my family saw me was when I turned up at my brother's graduation, having been previously assured I was safe. I was in the hospital for six or seven months. That hospital is the only place I've had a fantasy about blowing it up.

"A year ago I bought this house in the mountains, work about once a month in a band, worked until recently in a record-store. I'm fixing up the house, re-painting it. I've asked all my friends staying here to leave gradually. I want to be spiritually alone for a while.

"Out in the mountains drugs help you to get into the flow of the universe. I'm in Tao [pronounced "Tow"]. You are part of everything. I take LSD very occasionally. Next week I may go up into the mountains and take some pure LSD from Switzerland. You don't need much money here, and we all help each other."

His wife came into the shabby psychedelic living room with their two small children. She was a pretty girl with long shining black tresses and a somewhat hard look.

"I just came over," she said coldly, "to say the police are after the fifteen-year-old girl. Is she here?"

"I don't know," smiled Dave vaguely.

"Tell her to call her father now. She gets picked up for the third time and she goes into a juvenile home. That's where it's at."

"Keeping her away from her family is where it's at," replied David.

"I'm going to Cheyenne for a couple of days."

"Bye, Daddy," said the little boy and girl.

We went to The Aquarius, a health-food snack bar where the vegetables were flown in presumably free of chemicals from California. For lunch there was David, me, and Tarot, a jazz pianist, and Tarot's girl friend. David seemed to know half of the young people there. One of the owners was a Baba lover. Dave advised a couple of friends on where to get some bail money. "I like to be a center of communication," he confided.

Driving away afterward, a car pulled up beside us, and a hippie called urgently to Dave, "Call your father. The police are looking for that girl right now."

We parked on a side street. "She's got terrible parents."

"I'm going in to get rid of her stuff," said David lithely getting out of the car. He walked around the corner swinging his arms in half circles, bringing his hands together at the end of the double swoop.

"Marvel" then joined me and told me about a copy of *The Urantia Book* and another titled *A Treatise on Cosmic Fire* by Alice A. Bailey, a medium.

Urantia, a sort of Christo-centered, 2097 page long volume, "was taught at The Free University beside The University of Colorado," he said.

Back in the house—all safe—David and I chatted. Then he said, "I've got something to do for five minutes. Marvel will talk to you." Marvel, who had friendly yet hostile blue eyes, said that The Urantia teachings were without ritual or organization and therefore no one was excluded.

Whether David was upstairs with the runaway, or whether he had left with her, I did not know, and Marvel's and the two other commune visitors' remarks as to his whereabouts were vague.

I called, "David . . . David . . ." but once again David had disappeared. I wrote a note and left.

Note: "Ur Commune is not the actual name for the group described. All names, locations, the description of their buildings, and the personal characteristics of individuals, have been changed to prevent the identity of any living persons. The references to Meher Baba and the teachings of Alice A. Bailey and the Urantia book are actual.

CHAPTER VIII

Black
Muslims

Since I am white, it was impossible for me to interview the Black Muslims directly. Thus this chapter is dependent entirely on other sources—usually firsthand accounts by blacks of the fellow members of their race who belong to this highly publicized religion. Malcolm X—expelled and assassinated—was a member, as is Muhammad Ali (formerly Cassius Clay). Although the Black Muslims because of their anti-white stance and lower-income membership are quite different from the other new beliefs in this book, they share the same alienation from Majority America and sense of group security.

In his review of *The Black Muslims in America*, by C. Eric Lincoln, a black, Peter Kihss in *The New York Times Book Review* says they belong in the historical context of The Moorish Science Temples of Noble Drew Ali, started in 1913, and Marcus Garvey's "back to Africa" movement.

Starting in 1913, Noble Drew Ali, more of a religious leader than Garvey, founded a number of Moorish Science temples, giving a sense of identity to blacks by using nationality identification cards. He was mysteriously murdered.

Perhaps better known was Garvey, the important black political rebel of the early 1920s. He advocated a return to

Liberia, and won a large number of supporters. Garvey, who was originally from Jamaica, was deported by the U. S. government following his conviction on a weak charge of defrauding the mails. The parallels to Johnson, the exiled heavyweight champion, Eldridge Cleaver, and the prosecution of Muhammad Ali, who like Cleaver, faced criminal charges, are chilling.

In 1930 a man appeared in Detroit. He called himself Master Fard. He may possibly have been an Arab, but the details of his past are unclear. He began to recommend African foods to other blacks and tell stories of his adventures in other nations. He told them of their true African and Asian religion, attacking Christianity. After a while he started to denounce whites. His meetings became increasingly successful, and a hall was rented. This was the first Temple of Islam.

The new religion grew steadily over the next three years and then Fard gave up active leadership, leaving behind his organization. Fard disappeared, an event that has baffled everyone even up to the present day. Among the wild but unsubstantiated rumors were the ones that he had been murdered by the police, that he had been assassinated by some of his disciples, or that he had boarded a ship to Europe.

One of the officers was Elijah Muhammad from Georgia. His birth name was Elijah Poole. Muhammad was forced by moderates in the Detroit temple to move to another one in Chicago. There it was soon taught that Fard was deified as Allah, and Muhammad became his Prophet. Muhammad spent four years in American prisons from 1941 to 1946 "for exhorting his followers not to register for the draft," Lincoln says.

Although there was considerable growth under Muhammad, Lincoln, in his book, which is probably the definitive one on the Black Muslims, gives much of the credit for their expansion to Malcolm X. Malcolm joined the Muslims while in prison in the late Forties.

By 1959 membership of the Black Muslims had grown to

thirty thousand. Then Mike Wallace presented a TV documentary on the sect, and extensive newspaper and magazine coverage ensued. The numbers doubled. By 1961 it was estimated that there were sixty-nine temples and one hundred thousand followers in the U.S.

Probably the next important event in Muslim history was the death of Malcolm X, and the circumstances leading up to it. Malcolm was a dynamic, angry speaker with great persuasive powers, who attracted large numbers to the religion. He became even better known than Elijah Muhammad, and at the time of his demise had extensive contacts with whites, particularly among the members of the press.

It seems likely that a struggle for power and domination was a basic cause of the conflict between Malcolm X and Muhammad. The first specific issue between them was Malcolm's discovery of Muhammad's amorous affairs and illegitimate children. When the younger man discussed the matter with his leader they both agreed at the time that a prophet's good points were more important than his weaknesses. Muhammad offered the excuses that David in the Bible had slept with another man's wife and that Noah had become drunk and that Lot had slept with his own daughters. Muhammad was only fulfilling a prophecy. Malcolm X said that the reports of Muhammad's infidelities were filtering down through the hierarchy of the Muslims. Malcolm said he warned a few of the brothers not to be disturbed by their prophet's sexual life. According to Malcolm, Muhammad suspended him for giving these warnings. This was the real motivation, but the incident which enabled Muhammad to relieve Malcolm of his position was a political one, arising out of the death of President Kennedy. Malcolm X had said it was "a case of 'the chickens coming home to roost.'" There was horrified protest from white America, who, as I recall the event, interpreted the statement to mean that Kennedy had received what he deserved, whereas Malcolm meant that Kennedy was a victim of the violence which America had nurtured over the years and directed particularly against blacks.

In *The Autobiography of Malcolm X* he writes, "Three days later, the first word came to me that a Mosque Seven official who had been one of my most immediate assistants was telling certain Mosque Seven brothers: 'If you knew what the Minister did, you'd go out and kill him yourself.'

"And then I knew. As any official in the Nation of Islam would instantly have known, any death-talk for me could have been approved of—if not actually initiated—by only one man."

Since Malcolm's murder it appears there has been little, if any growth, in the number of Muslims.

In order to join the Black Muslims a potential member must write a perfectly-spelled letter of submission to Muhammad. He gives up his last name, inherited through his ancestors from a white slave owner, and adds "X" which means formerly "Jones" or "Smith" or whatever the white-inherited surname was. If there is more than one member in a temple with the same first name, a number precedes the "X" to distinguish them. "X" has a secondary meaning of rebirth and mystery for the past, before slavery. The mystery will not be cleared up for whites until enough blacks are converted to counter the white man's treatment over hundreds of years.

The early morning routine of a Muslim tells something about the way of life which a new member will experience. For Malcolm X it was a radical change from the confusion he had previously known in most homes. The man of the house arises and washes first. Then his wife, and then the children. "In the name of Allah, I perform the ablution," says the man before washing his right hand and then his left. He brushes his teeth carefully and rinses his mouth three times. He washes out his nostrils three times. Then he takes a shower.

The members of the family say to each other first "As—Salaam—Alaikum" and then answer "Wa—Alaikum—Salaam." Like the endlessly repetitive praying of the Hare Krishna or the meditative repetition of the Maharishi's mantra the man repeats in his brain, "Allaha—Akbar," meaning "Allah is the greatest."

Wearing gowns, the family removes their sandals, moves onto a prayer rug, directing themselves toward the East, and prays. Malcolm X says he and his brother Wilfrid had only coffee and juice for breakfast.

Before entering the temple for services, which occur about twice a week, Muslims are "frisked" for weapons. Inside, the men sit on the right and the women on the left. The first activity is sometimes a speech by a Muslim brother explaining an Arabic word or teaching the congregation how to pray, facing the East with their palms turned up.

When the minister enters, he says "As—Salaam—Alaikum," which means "Peace be unto you!" The people reply "Wa—Alaikum—Salaam," meaning "And unto you be peace!" The minister addresses them about the entire body of Muslim teaching, rather than concentrating on one doctrine. Guards are walking up and down and changing places rhythmically. Singing is absent, and the main response of the Muslims is "That's right!" for a strong statement by the speaker. If he should ask a rhetorical question embarrassing to the hated whites, they may snicker, "Now that's a good question, Brother Minister!"

In most temples there is a painting. On one side of it are the star and crescent of Islam. On the other side are the Cross, the American flag and a black hanging from a tree. In the attack on Christianity, it is pointed out that whites seduce blacks into becoming Christians and then laugh at them (see Baha''i', Chapter II, for a similar criticism of Christian hypocrisy).

To prove black supremacy, the minister will quote from the Islamic Quaron, the Old Testament, and other sources, including Muhammad's writings. History notes the fact that Aesop was a black and that the famous University of Sankore in Timbuktu had visiting lecturers teaching in the educational centers of Morocco, Granada, and Cairo when Europe was just coming out of the Dark Ages.

Near the end of a meeting, questions from the congregation are answered. People who want to give up Christianity and become Muslims are urged to come forward. Individuals, who are uncertain, are invited to come to more meetings. Curiosity-seekers are not invited again, nor are those suspected of being F.B.I. agents.

The Muslims' stern code of morality is well-known. They pray toward Mecca five times a day, and abstain from pork and tobacco. Muslims must proselytize in the street, and dislike marriage outside of the Muslim faith, abhorring particularly adultery and liaisons with whites. The Fruit of Islam is the elite Muslim security force composed of strong young men. One of their tasks is protecting Muhammad. Punishment administered by the FOI consists mainly of labor at the temple or varying lengths of expulsion, if not permanent dismissal.

According to an article in *Ebony* Magazine, August, 1970, "Although pledged to obedience to their husbands and fathers, women are held in esteem as bearers of the black nation's future." There are more male than female members, but Lincoln says Muslim women like the security of this approach (combined undoubtedly with the steadfastness of the home life), and that Muslim children are never delinquents. Young Muslims have been especially successful in working with young drug addicts and bringing them back to an effective life.

Muslims attempt to protect their arrested brothers by appearing en masse at police stations where they are taken. In addition, Muslim proselytizers are young, energetic, personable, persuasive, and masculine. The emphasis on male strength, ego, and identity is important for black men so long humiliated by whites and before the eyes of black women.

The strict order of Muslim life seems particularly effective for former convicts who have lived an anarchic, amoral life of drugs, alcohol, and illicit sex. Interestingly enough a convict-convert, of which Malcolm X was an example, is trained to respect authority, even in jail. Their record in prison improves. The Muslims have been particularly suc-

cessful in recruiting ex-criminals. An ex-con is often given a
job in a Muslim business. James Baldwin in *The Fire Next
Time* credits them with helping, among others, junkies
and drunkards. He says they have given pride to black men
and women—unlike Christainity.

The Black Muslims operate parochial schools. Arabic is
taught. In the past there have been various attempts by
local government officials to close them, but these have usually failed.

Where do the Muslims seek new members? In jails. In
bars and pool halls. In drugstores and barbershops. On college campuses and in YMCAs. Young, confident, and well-
dressed, they often speak on street corners. They pass out
literature. Their official weekly newspaper, *Muhammad
Speaks*, has a circulation of six hundred thousand. It is
claimed that each male sells an average of three hundred per
week at fifteen cents a copy, which would raise the circulation considerably above that.

They have a number of talented musicians and they perform plays. A popular Muslim play features a white man
who is prosecuted, found guilty, and sentenced to death.
The black audience applauds.

The Muslims hire a few whites in their businesses when
positions can't be filled with qualified blacks, admitting with
apparent glee that "quite a few white devils are helping
us." Recently the Muslims have been emphasizing economic expansion and own a wide variety of businesses, including restaurants, farms, clothing stores, food canning
plants, and grocery markets. They farm four thousand, two
hundred acres in Michigan, Georgia, and Alabama. *Time*,
March 7, 1969, says their stores have names like "The
Shabazz Kosher Market," "The Kaaba Haberdashery," and
"Omar's Ice Cream Parlor." Their increasing interest in
economic growth and the conceded hiring, even temporarily, of whites indicates that the Muslim opposition to
white America may not be as total as it was earlier.

There are "forty Black Muslim temples and mosques
across the nation," according to *Ebony* with one hundred

thousand followers. The Black Muslims' rapid growth has been generally accepted by much of the guilt-ridden white liberal press. But C. Eric Lincoln in *The Black Muslims in America*, published in 1961, stated there were sixty-nine temples and one hundred thousand followers in the U.S. then. H. J. Massaquoi, the writer of the *Ebony* article, implies that young blacks "are not turning to Islam in sufficiently significant numbers to signal a national trend," because of the strict rules and Moslem ritual. Since Malcolm X's death there seems to have been little, if any, growth. The various outsiders who have been in contact with the Muslims indicate that no successor to Elijah Muhammad is being groomed.

In the early part of the Sixties their membership appears to have been about eighty percent young, ranging in age from seventeen to thirty-five. Many of the older members previously belonged to the Garvey or Noble Drew Ali movements. Usually their temples and mosques are in the poorer parts of the ghettos. With few exceptions the Muslims are American Negroes. In the Garvey movement there were considerable numbers of Jamaicans. However, the Muslims are not as interested in Jamaicans because of the island people's custom of making distinctions between lighter- and darker-skinned blacks. There is a possible class difference between the intellectual black who becomes independent, who may join Baha"i' (see Chapter II), but stays within the system, and the Muslim who defiantly and wholeheartedly repudiates all of white America.

Muhammad, who is now seventy-three, lives in a nineteen-room mansion-cum-office on the edge of a black slum on the Southside of Chicago. Urban renewal is planned for the area. The interior is said to be unostentatious, almost austere. On television one black commentator described Muhammad as being a small man, lacking presence. He described his voice as being "thin, asthmatic." He accused him of possessing a special talent for breaking grammatical rules in his speeches. However, in person the same critic found Muhammad charming and warm with a delightful smile. He takes the visitor's hand with both hands. This recent impression is supported by Baldwin's account of his visit to the headquarters. Before meeting Muhammad he "associated him with ferocity. But, no—the man who came into the room was small and slender, really very delicately put together, with a thin face, large, warm eyes, and a most winning smile." Baldwin noticed, too, the joy that went back and forth between Muhammad and his followers. There is a considerable contrast between the slight build of the leader and the muscular appearance of the young guards who surround Muhammad.

An important figure in the Muslim hierarchy is Supreme Captain Raymond Sharrieff, who often heads the FOI bodyguard surrounding Muhammad. Yet another significant figure is Minister Louis X of the Boston Temple Number Eleven. Five of Muhammad's six sons work in the administration center in Chicago.

Their philosophy is worthy of study. The Black Muslims teach that "Original Man" appeared at the time of the "Big Bang." This explosion separated the earth from the moon sixty-six trillion years ago. These first men were blacks, and the American Negro is a direct descendant. They settled in the Nile Valley and the area of the Middle East that is now known as Mecca and its environs. One of their number was "Yakub," a brilliant but evil genius, who wanted to destroy the other blacks. He cross-bred the weaker lighter-skinned blacks, producing black and brown germs. Over several hundred years on the island of Pelan (or Patmos) (*The New York Times*, January 13, 1969) the yellow and other races were developed. Eventually by this degenerating process, the white strain was evolved. The fact that whites have no blackness shows them to be destined for death. Whites are only six thousand years old.

The phrase, the "Lost Nation of Islam," means that blacks were lost when they were sold into slavery in America. However, Allah has sent a messenger to rescue them from the white man's corruption. He is Elijah Muhammad. They say that black Christian ministers have deceived their

flocks. The white man, who is incurably sick, is aware that
blacks are natural leaders.

Muslims support peace among blacks, but oppose it for
whites. Caucasians are contemptuous of blacks. They claim
it is impossible to love a man who hates you. Christianity
for them is unrealistic.

The opposition to Christian symbols and the absence of
peace and love in their dogma, at least as in regard to the
white man, can be interpreted as both the strength and
weakness of the Black Muslim religion. Although it satisfies
the justified rage of non-whites in this country against their
masters, this warlike attitude, this hatred, undoubtedly
repels many blacks who might otherwise consider joining
the Muslims. Malcolm X was trying to modify this teaching; possibly it was one of the causes of his downfall. Yet, as
is hinted in their growing accommodation to white American standards of materialism, a policy of less rigid opposition may diminish their appeal to the very strong feelings
of dislike in the black community for whites. Another fac-
tor that lessens their attractiveness to some blacks is the
strict Muslim policy of separatism.

Typical of the Muslim position on race is the following
statement from Elijah Muhammad: "Since we cannot get
along with our former slave masters in peace and equality
after giving them four hundred years of our sweat and
blood and receiving in return some of the worst treatment
human beings have ever experienced, we believe our contributions to this land and the suffering forced upon us by
white America justifies our demand for complete separation
in a state or territory of our own."

Muhammad predicted the destruction of the whites by
war in ten years. However, *Time* on August 10, 1959, reported that "The Muslims" were calling 1970 "their D-
Day" when atomic warfare between white nations would
have eliminated them, and Black Africa will stand unchal-
lenged.

In his beautifully written, very interesting essay, *The
Fire Next Time*, Baldwin describes what he thinks would

be a logical Black Muslim fantasy, whereby the U.S. would no longer be a world power, whereby the Muslims would have six or seven Southern states, whereby an unfriendly Latin America (including the Muslim territory) would now be on the border of Maryland. Europe would be impotent. The East would be dangerous. The Russians would be waiting on the Alaskan border.

At another point in his treatise Baldwin describes Elijah Muhammad's effect on him, saying he felt as if he "was back in my father's house . . ."

CHAPTER IX

Witchcraft

As witches are extremely secretive (one of the reasons being the persecution they suffered in past centuries), information is very difficult to obtain. It is very rare that an outsider may attend a coven, the Scottish and Old French word for "a company or assembly; specifically a coven of witches." Witchcraft is a very old pre-Christian religion which has been almost completely suppressed by zealous clerics (e.g. the deaths of Joan of Arc and the witches in the Salem, Massachusetts, trials)—until its recent, modest revival.

A well-known British witch and medium, Sybil Leek, says that five years ago in the U.S. there were two hundred and eighty covens (twelve witches to a coven), today there are four hundred. Young people are particularly interested in witchcraft. One hundred twenty-five students, for example, took a course, "Witchcraft, Magic and Sorcery," at New York University's School of Continuing Education. The movie, *Rosemary's Baby*, has a witchcraft theme. *Bewitched*, the TV series, features a good witch, Samantha.

The coven usually consists of six men and six women with a high priest or priestess. They believe in reincarnation. "Witchcraft," says Miss Leek, "is a return to a native religion" [the 'Old Religion']. It gives people their place in the universe and helps them see religion much more clearly . . . a religion that acknowledges them as human beings."

At a meeting on Long Island, the witches open proceedings by saying, "Blessed be." These monthly gatherings are called "esbats." Throughout the year there are eight festivals known as "sabbats," one of which is Halloween. Invariably the high priest or priestess gives a recitation from "The Book of Shadows," their equivalent of the Bible. This volume describes their rites, cures, charms, and spells.

In New York City, Mr. Raymond Buckland, a leader of the Long Island group, speaking with a middle-class English accent, described to an audience of unenthusiastic kids in the two-thirds empty Fillmore East the initiation of a new witch into the coven. On the screen behind him were flashed photos of their rites, including the high priestess. She had attractive breasts and long black hair sometimes covering them. This was at the first and probably last Occult Festival. He talked about sacred knives and blindfolding and a boar's head. It struck me that their witchcraft ceremonies devoted to the free life were more tease than action. Mr. Buckland, a hair-slicked gentleman slightly ill at ease on the shabby stage, undoubtedly made some money out of telling about his religion (so do Catholic priests and Norman Vincent Peale).

In an interview a few weeks later in a crowded restaurant in midtown Manhattan, Mr. Buckland said I could not be told of the details of their magic.

"Tradition," he said. "Curing—mental and physical—is the usual secret practice. Silence, except at the Beginning and End. The cousin of a witch, paralyzed after a car accident, appeared on crutches in one of our member's driveway, walking for the first time. . . . Another member, who lives in Patchogue, Long Island, had a neighbor whose kids were a great nuisance to him. We used magic to urge him to leave. We did not hurt him. Yes, it was a bit presumptuous. The man returned to Brooklyn, saying 'The area's too quiet for my kids.' "

The theory behind witchcraft seems to be the pooling of bodily forces (thus, the nudity). There are no sexual acts in the Buckland coven, though Hans Holzer in his book, *The Truth about Witchcraft,* reported witches making love during advanced rituals in a London, England, coven. "In all my years in witchcraft I've seen an erection no more often than the fingers of one hand. I feel no embarrassment over my or my wife's nudity," said Buckland.

His great grandfather was a gypsy. "There is close similarity between their religion and witchcraft." He agreed that witchcraft was "a religion of freedom, joy in the sensual appetites and in nature." About fifty years old, he had a goatee, was a small, rather neatly-dressed dapper man. There were dark rings under his eyes and the lids hung over them. "I've been working late at night on a book." He earns ten thousand dollars a year as an editor; last year he made three to four thousand dollars from writing and lecturing on witchcraft, and hopes to make eight thousand on the side this year. Though he answered my questions very openly (except for the magical aspects), his tone of voice was always emotionless. He was hoping to give up his job, sell their fourteen-thousand-dollar ranch-style house (now worth twenty to twenty-five thousand in the suburb of Brentwood, Long Island) and move his wife and two boys, ages twelve (he is a witch) and ten (he is not), to a place in Cooperstown, New York, where he will have a witchcraft museum.

Buckland recommends especially two books—*The God of the Witches* by Margaret A. Murray, a noted English scholar, and *Witchcraft Today* by Gerald B. Gardner, "a member of one of the ancient covens of the Witch Cult which still survives in England." Miss Murray was formerly Assistant Professor in Egyptology at University College, London. Her book is historical and academic, and traces "the worship of the Horned God from palaeolithic times to the medieval period." She argues that Joan of Arc, Gilles de Rais, Thomas à Becket and William Rufus were priest-kings destined to rule for a certain period and then to be ritually killed so that a successor could reign. Gardner's book is more up-to-date and British-oriented, explaining among other things the origin of the broomstick and the role of "the priestess acting as the Moon Goddess."

The service in the Bucklands' basement begins with the witches taking off their clothes, becoming "skyclad," and immersing themselves in saltwater as a form of purification. Naked, they go down to the cellar and enter a nine-foot circle which is outlined for the other witches by Mrs. Buckland using a sword four hundred years old. Mrs. Buckland is called "Lady Rowen." Music comes from a tape recorder while incense burns in a brass censer.

Within the circle the witches sing, chant, and dance, using broomsticks to symbolize an old fertility ceremony. They consume wine and tea, and hear the words spoken by Lady Rowen from *The Book of Shadows*.

Lady Rowen, wearing a necklace, a green leather garter, a bracelet and a silver crown, puts a horned helmet on Raymond's head. He is called "Robat." The crowning ceremony means that he will reign during the six months of winter, whereas she has reigned during the summer's half-year. This concludes the service.

Buckland and his wife describe themselves as "white," or good witches; the late Dr. Gardner initiated them into the Craft in 1962 on the Isle of Man near England. Mrs. Buckland says they believe that the good or bad one does will return three fold in the afterlife.

The New York Times in an article on October 31, 1969, ran a photo of a Mrs. Florence S, who lives in Brooklyn, stroking a black cat called Thirteen. When she and her husband sail on Long Island Sound, Florence, who is a witch, stands up in the boat and cries "Carabouch," requesting Carabouch to ask the gentle sisters of the West and South to send a wind, which usually appears. She claimed to have used her powers on Kevin, a young ice skater, who subsequently won all his skating tournaments. To her friends she gives black stones, called gagis, for good luck charms. She promised a single woman that if the spinster gave one to the man of her choice he would marry her. She claims her house is haunted by a female ghost who resides in a linen closet (I couldn't help wondering whether the spirit needed a ready supply of ghostly sheets when going out). One day the spirit prevented her from tumbling down the stairs to the basement. Once, she said, she tried black magic, but lost her powers for a year.

Holzer's book, though overly detailed, and containing the built-in restriction from at least one coven that he would print nothing unfavorable about them, is written in a lively and sympathetic style, and gives a considerable amount of concrete information. However, in most cases he was unable to print surnames. Specific rituals and beliefs vary to some degree from coven to coven. In the London group during the initiation of a new member there is a ceremony of kissing the penis and vagina, but in a brief stylized manner.

In the U.S. Holzer discovered a coven in Cincinnati, Ohio, consisting of thirteen members. They use some aspects of a Greek Dionysian cult, and worship Baphomet who is also a God of the Knight Templars. Their leader blesses wine and says, "Yod He Vau He, Blessed Be!" which in Hebrew represents Jehovah. He discovered another coven in Pasadena, a suburb of Los Angeles, and still another led by one Fred and Martha elsewhere in Los Angeles.

Holzer also describes a number of individuals who practice witchcraft privately and yet others of a somewhat spurious nature who emphasize the commercial aspect. He distinguishes between witchcraft and satanism, in which the devil is worshiped. This is *not* the practice in witchcraft. He also points out how many of the people involved in witchcraft have other psychic powers, such as precognition.

For a religion with no central organization, witches flourish surprisingly well. Forced to remain secret by opposition from most Americans, they face extreme prejudice. The Cincinnati group has "lately been hounded by prejudiced neighbors, and their temple had to be closed." In the summer of 1970 the witches of New York held a "witch-in" in Central Park, dancing on the green of the Sheep Meadow and demanding the freedom to worship openly. But to some extent, their desire for exclusivity is motivated by the knowledge that witchcraft may be the one thing that distinguishes them from their neighbors.

CHAPTER X

Rumors and
Reports of Religions

In a changing world with such rapidly growing movements, it is obviously impossible to give each subject the scope which it deserves. To write of potentially hundreds of these religions, or even to trace them (or for that matter to note those that are dying), would be impractical.

The following are rumors of a few of the new beliefs, although a number of them have been substantiated to some degree:

"Surfing" in California—where else—is now regarded by some of its young advocates as a mystical experience, for them the center of the wave becomes a oneness with the universe. But how new is this concept? According to *The New York Times* of May 10, 1970, "In Hindu and Buddhist thought . . . the wave is a symbol of the individual who rises to life, and then disappears back into the universal oneness of reality."

There are some farmers—from the youth culture scene—who meditate, pray, "dance and chant in an effort to benefit their crops." This from *The New York Times* of May 31, 1970. However, there are some organic farmers and commune hippies who are adopting the American Indian religious beliefs. A young hippie told me that the older Indians in New Mexico are introducing members of the communes into Indian religions which use peyote. He noted that the younger and middle-aged Indians sided with the Spanish-Americans, or "Chicanos," in their general dislike of hippies.

The Kou Ch'ien Institute, of the "four- and eight-hour 'Creative Meetings,'" ran an ad in *The Village Voice* on May 8, 1969. The same paper ran another ad for "The Unified Family" who offered "Lectures and discussion" on "God's nature in the world today. Questions and answers our generation seeks." According to reports, "The Unified Family" is a sort of religious commune located at 1611 Upshur Street, N.W., in Washington, D.C.

The young man called "Portnoy" at the Baba center in Myrtle Beach, South Carolina, said, "There is a group called Kirpalsingh who are Indian in their beliefs located at Heildsburgh, ninety miles south of Sacramento, California."

A psychic named Deziah Rhodes who lives in New York City says she gives classes in "Huna, the study of the religion of magic from Hawaii."

A publicity release informs us that Sri Paul Twitchell is the spiritual leader of *Eckankar,* or the Ancient Science of Soul Travel, which he learned at an early age in India, together with his stepsister. According to the publicity release *Eckankar* has five hundred thousand followers and Twitchell receives six thousand to ten thousand letters weekly and personally answers at least sixteen thousand of them a year. Twitchell made a miraculous appearance last year before a group of young Czechoslovakians who were demonstrating on the first anniversary of the invasion. His headquarters were noted at Las Vegas, Nevada, although he lives on the West Coast and has a retreat in Mexico.

Supposedly there is the "Stelle Group" in Chicago, which publishes a book, *The Ultimate Frontier,* but I was unable to locate them there.

Outside of Santa Fe, New Mexico, on Route 285, there may be a new hippie Buddhist-type temple.

Some mention should be made of Alan Watts, who attracts very large numbers of young people to his talks on

Eastern beliefs, and Krishnamurti, whose career extends all the way back to Annie Besant of Theosophy. Krishnamurti is strongly opposed to religious teachers and organizations. Thousands of young people listen to Watts's words, and millions have read his books, according to Needleman.

Esperitismo is now popular with some black and Spanish-speaking people. It dates back to African beliefs and Caribbean voodoo, and emphasizes, among other things, curses which are delivered in exact detail. There are Esperitismo shops or botanicas in Puerto Rican sections of New York City selling candles of various colors which promise love, money, or evil wishes to the buyer. There are many Esperitismo mediums working out of storefronts, botanicas, and apartment rooms, who will give advice for fees ranging from two to five dollars.

CALIFORNIA

California has always been, and it remains, a fertile spawning ground for new religions.

It was in Los Angeles that Charles Manson was brought to trial for murder. Although I did not search for Satanic Cultists, I did not hear of a single such group mentioned among the hundreds of people—both young and old—whom I interviewed. Hans Holzer, the authority on witchcraft, in discussing Manson and the so-called satanic group in a televised interview, said, "there is no historical background for any Satanic Cult. It is a new invention."

Nevertheless a few such individuals do exist.

Jean Stafford in *McCall's* (March, 1970) wrote that Manson gave "himself the courtesy title of God and Satan . . . Jesus, the visible manifestation of God."

On April 13, 1970, *Newsweek* reported that there is "San Francisco's Church of Satan." Its head, Anton LeVey, gives a service which the magazine's reporter described as "a highly stylized arcane bore." LeVey claims there are "seven thousand fee-paying members."

In the March, 1970, issue of *Esquire* there is a more lurid portrait. Tom Burke discovered a woman doing a satanic dance in a Los Angeles nightclub called "The Climax." He later attended a party in the woman's house where she held a black swan between her thighs. The woman said subsequently "that three years ago" she had been "a Clairol-blonded hausfrau."

Would five thousand be a wild guess as to the number of Satanic Cultists in the U.S. in 1970?

The following individual is illustrative of the countless numbers of people among the two hundred million Americans spread across the continent now active in the new religions. I met with him for forty-five minutes after one brief telephone call, in which I tried unsuccessfully to trace another holy man known as "Sufi Sam." It was our fate to meet then. We will probably never meet again.

He had dark eyebrows, gray wavy hair, brown Persian skin, and a beautiful profile. He talked in soft educated tones, occasionally glancing at me with a slight grin, as for example, when he said, "We are going beyond the physical world into another world—and beyond that—in mysticism today." (The physical world was intruding on him in that he was suffering from a bout of flu.) His name was Pir Vilayat Khan. He was staying for a few days at a "commune" in San Francisco, located in a neat low-middle-income district on Precita Avenue, where several young couples lived who were practitioners of Sufism.

One of his young American disciples, who had changed his name to the more exotic "Wali Ali," told me, "There have been many communes. But we noticed those lasted longest which had a religious spiritual base."

Khan said, "I come to America four times a year. My home is in Paris. I travel so much now I rarely see my wife."

"They [referring to the Sufi mystics] don't believe what they see. Mysticism is the experience where nothing exists except God," said Wali.

"What is happening now," said Khan in his dulcet voice, "is that all religions are coming together in the unity of

God. On Sunday there will be six of us at The Persian Cat—Yogi Bhajan, Swamiji, myself, Steve Gaskin . . ." (The Persian Cat is a large San Francisco dance hall which is run as a "commune"; the meeting was advertised as a "Holy Man Jam.")

"Gaskin is a sort of Leary—psychedelics and the spirit—popular in San Francisco.

"I've been coming to the U.S. for six or seven years. I will go to the East-West Cultural Center in Los Angeles, a center in San Jacinto, California, and the Blaisdell Institute located outside of Los Angeles. In Tucson, Arizona, I will be at a youth camp where there will be about one hundred people from eighteen to thirty years of age."

". . . who've come to see Pir Vilayat," said Wali.

"I've been to the Unity Church in Chicago, Indianapolis, and Seattle. On my last trip I went to New York, Washington, Houston, Dallas, and Denver."

The brochure of "Pir Vilayat Khan's Second Annual U. S. Youth Camp" says it will last a week in "Paradise, Arizona, (one hundred and fifty miles east of Tucson) . . . The nearest store is sixty miles away over a dirt road . . . Hot days, warm nights." The sheet says, "Camp activity will include training in meditation, development of inner faculties, Dervish dancing, group counseling (with the aim of lifting the mask of the ego in order to see 'the Eternal Face' radiating thru the personality), devotional singing, lectures by Pir Vilayat, utilization of the natural talents of those present whatever they might be, freedom . . ." Those present will also sleep in tents and eat "vegetarian meals." It notes that a motion-picture crew will be filming the camp's activities, but they will be required to become integrated with the life of the camp and not allowed to remain hidden in the role of observers.

"Any questions can be sent to the above address. God willing, this second camp will manifest the same miracle of love that all who were present in Colorado last year remember so vividly."

PART II

The Indian Religions

CHAPTER XI

Transcendental Meditation: The Spiritual Regeneration Movement

Maharishi Mahesh Yogi completed a session of training three hundred and seventy teachers of Transcendental Meditation in December, 1970, at the YMCA of the Rockies. His book, *The Science of Being and Art of Living*, three hundred and thirty-five pages long, constantly emphasizing the discovery of Being through Transcendental Meditation, "or controlled thinking," contains sentences such as the following (selected at random) :

"The appreciation of activity from the gross outer to the subtle inner levels of perception is obviously the path in the inward direction."

"If the existence of the supreme, almighty, personal God cannot be intellectually conceived of, it would appear to be the result of poor understanding."

The answer to all problems—political, educational, psychological, sociological—is Transcendental Meditation.

The Maharishi considers it outrageous to inform a person that his life is built on bad treatment of that individual in earlier years. He wants the world's political leaders to understand the deleterious effects of psychoanalysis and to promote instead Transcendental Meditation.

The Maharishi's views on child-raising:

"Children have to be nurtured in love, and they have to

be punished if they are wrong in order to help them to succeed in life at all levels."

In the appendix of the book are statements from an Italian member of parliament and nineteen Indian M.P.'s advocating the Maharishi's methods for attaining world harmony and happiness.

Simplistic, soporific for the untutored, but soothing, the Maharishi's message is clearly a boon to some of the world's population.

An article in *Science*, March 27, 1970, titled "Physiological effects of Transcendental Meditation" by Robert Keith Wallace, of the Department of Physiology, School of Medicine, Center for the Health Sciences, Los Angeles, begins: "Abstract. *Oxygen consumption, heart rate, skin resistance, and electroencephalograph measurements were recorded before, during, and after subjects practiced a technique called transcendental meditation. There were significant changes between the control period and the meditation period in all measurements. During the meditation, oxygen consumption and heart rate decreased, and the electro-encephalogram showed specific changes in certain frequencies. These results seem to distinguish the state produced by transcendental meditation from commonly encountered states of consciousness and suggest that it may have practical applications.*"

The book concludes with the fact that Transcendental Meditation can be easily learned and may produce significant physiological changes in both beginners and advanced students, giving it certain advantages over other, more austere techniques.

"Approximately one hundred and twenty-five thousand people practice Transcendental Meditation in the U.S.," said Charles F. Lutes, president of the Spiritual Regeneration Movement Foundation of America, the Maharishi's organization in the U.S. A beginner is given a secret word chosen by his instructor, called a "mantra," and told to repeat this over and over to himself nonverbally within his brain for a period of twenty minutes daily. The resultant calm and psychological uplift is somewhat comparable to the Roman Catholic repetition of the prayer, "Hail Mary."

At the S.R.M. Center in New York City business was clearly off, although Charles Lutes detected "an upswing again." Mr. Lutes was fifty-four, president of S.R.M., and its subsidiary, I.T.M.S., International Transcendental Meditation Society, a sales representative for a large manufacturer, who was making seven or eight hundred dollars a month eleven years ago. "When I first met Maharishi," he said, lifting and waving his hands frequently like the Swamis. Otherwise he was a one hundred percent American businessman, dressed in a conservative blue suit, neat tie and starched collar, with his hair slightly graying and immaculately cut. "I'd been to a lot of these Yoga people before, and they never made any sense with remarks like 'The Manifestation of the self un-manifests itself through the manifestation of the being.' Maharishi was simple, and spoke English you could understand. Some men go to a bar or to the Elks in the evening. For me it's the Maharishi. I was very nervous and tense for about two years. You could say I'd had a breakdown. After a few months of meditation my tension had gone." Married, Mr. Lutes is from Los Angeles.

OKLAHOMA

In Jo's ground-floor apartment surrounded by trees and bushes she had posters and paintings on her walls of Maharishi, the Beatles that were—George Harrison—the one who went to India—and the pop singer, Donovan. Her own paintings were sinuous and abstract. There was one by her boyfriend—a mosaic and more complex than hers. They had gone together for three years. She was five-feet-six inches tall with rather large breasts for her otherwise slim body. She had hazel eyes and long blonde hair and wore a mini-dress with an Eastern-looking pattern which she had purchased somewhere in Oklahoma.

Said Hank, her long-haired, immaculate boyfriend, "We

haven't made love more than twice immediately after meditating, which we must have done more than six hundred times. In fact you make love less after you start meditating as you don't have to in order to release tensions or hang-ups."

"When you do, it's because you really want to and not to relieve a hang-up," said Jo.

"The last time I meditated—yesterday," said Hank in his Brooklyn accent, "I became aware of my heart, the blood pumping, the arteries leading up to the brain. Each time the blood surged in I was more aware of everything around me."

"It's nice to meditate with someone else. You feel warm and close towards those around you," said Jo.

They are members of "SIMS—Student International Meditation Society," at a university in Oklahoma. In "SIMS" and the adult groups of the Maharishi's organization there are about two hundred and fifty members. They meet twice a week in a largish room in a student center on the Spanish-style campus where there have been recent bomb threats following a police attack which hospitalized many students.

Steve, the initiator (instructor) for the group, wearing a business suit, who was a recruiter for the Peace Corps, said, grinning, "The word you are given—your mantra—helps you to go out to subtler planes." He had returned from India several years before.

Later, as we walked across the campus to get the address of the Yoga group from the administrative office, I said to Jo, "Are you and Hank going to get married?"

"I don't think so. I'm going away after graduation. So we're going to be separated."

She then added brightly, "My parents are going to join ITMS. My father's in the consular service in the Middle East. At our meetings we meditate silently for about fifteen minutes and then rap. There's a lot of joy," said Jo.

Note: The above names and locations have been altered.

ARIZONA

In a city in Arizona, the local head of I.T.M.S. said, "The Maharishi told me, 'I want you to come to India and study.' I replied, 'Maharishi, I can't just drop everything.' He laughed. 'You will. You will.' So I quit my job as an executive and I didn't even tell them why, only that I was going around the world.

"At the beginning here it was more older people. But a lot of students have been joining and I would say the average age is late twenties, early thirties. We have several teachers, two doctors, a lawyer, many housewives, investment people, clerks and nurses.

"I was never a particularly sexual person, and of course it calms down as you get older, but since starting Maharishi it's quietened even more.

"I'm more conservative politically now since beginning meditating, but I don't want to overemphasize this. There hasn't been much change. I definitely support our President in Cambodia. That's the quickest way to end the war." When I asked him, "Why is that?" I could see that he did not want to discuss politics. He excused himself for a moment but soon returned.

He was in his fifties and a little above medium height, with curly white hair, tan skin, a fairly stocky but not overweight body. He wore glasses with black frames and a thin large gold wristwatch. He started to speak.

"One day a boy came in. He was about twenty years old and had been in a hospital for four months from methadrine or something like that. He acted in a daze and spoke in a faltering, barely audible voice. His friends had visited him, and said 'Save the money you're spending here on hospital bills and get initiated in meditation.'

"After I had given him his mantra and left him to meditate, I came back and his face was covered with tears.

" 'What's wrong?' I said.

" 'They're tears of happiness. It's such a relief. I feel I've come home,' he replied.

"Three months later—we had him checked a month after to see if he was still meditating—he called me and he was talking as naturally as I am now."

Downtown, the meditation room of I.T.M.S. was covered in thick red-pile carpet with soft cushions and there was subdued light.

A successful meditation means going down deeper and deeper. Each time one wants to stop there is an encounter with "a knot, a frustration which is being untied. I feel so happy. I don't miss my job, career, or the competition at all."

The sixteen people in the room—from a teen-ager to a nervous elderly lady—were mainly women dressed in a sporty fashion, sitting cross-legged on the cushions or on the green-cushioned benches. It was a lovely soft room designed by an Arizona architect and one of which the local head was justly pleased.

There was silence and the room was in near darkness. Two candles flickered beneath Maharishi's picture, illuminating the flowers placed in front of it. Some of the people fidgeted, but were usually calm with closed eyes, repeating their own mantra endlessly in their minds.

A rather charming all-American-type housewife with a sweet smiling quiescent chubby husband urged "everyone who's interested to come to the speakers' course next week."

Anthony, who looked like an ex-hippie not entirely reconciled to being a "square," read from the *Bhagavad Gita*. We then listened to a taped lecture on purity in meditation from Mahesh Yogi, elaborating in ever-widening ripples this simple message of love.

CHAPTER XII

Yoga

The number of Yogis and the different systems they offer—
Hatha, Karma, Bhakti, Raja, Japa, and Jnana—are almost
as infinite in the U.S. today as the manifestations of Krishna
and Vishnu. The Hare Krishna religion, the Maharishi's
meditation society, and Meher Baba belong to the same
Vedantic school of thought as the yogis, but I have written
about them separately. Among those covered in this chapter
are Yogiraz Sri Swami Satchidananda, whose base is New
York City, and Yogi Bhajan, whose headquarters are in Los
Angeles.

Yoga is popular among California surfers. Many of the
young Yoga students are physically attractive, particularly
the girls, and there seem to be a large proportion of actors
and actresses.

In New York City there is the Sivananda Ashram at 205
East 77th Street, and the Yogi Gupta Association at 150
East 50th Street. The New York *Village Voice* carries ads
for "Swami Jyotir Maya Nanda, the Genius of Yoga."
There is the Satnam Barge at Port Richmond on Staten
Island. Near Taos, I visited a tumbled down Ashram occu-
pied by hippies who were following Bhajan. (The competition must be rough; I wouldn't want to be in a room where
competing Yogis were practicing their supernatural powers
on each other.) In Los Angeles there are said to be follow-

ers of Paramahansa Yogananda. "Paramahansa Yogananda announced he was leaving this life," a Yoga student told me, "and his body remained uncorrupted for twenty days until the authorities came. He had not had an illness but just left."

From your reporter at the University of Texas:

The president of the student body at one time was rumored to be active in a yin-yang group. The Yoga practitioners met in a karate studio until it went bankrupt. Now, somewhat inactive, their leader, Rodman Thompson, a nutritionist, "hopes to get it going again in the fall." He had been a follower of Yogananda.

Yogi Bhajan has from "ten to thirty thousand" followers in the U.S. "He gives ten classes a week in the Topango Canyon area in California," said one of his disciples, a girl with a drawn face, who implied that Yogi had rescued her from a breakdown. In a Yoga room, doors open to the street, on a summer Saturday afternoon she chanted:

"Ek Ong Kar Sat Nam Siri Wha Guru.

"It's Sanskrit. It means One Creator [Ek] who creates this creation [Ong Kar], Truth [Sat], His Name [Nam] There's Nothing Greater [Siri Wha] than the Teacher [Guru]."

At her encouragement I rose at five A.M. to visit a "Holy Man Jam" in a public park near Dodger Stadium in Los Angeles. The "Holy Man Jam" in Elysian Park was a fiasco, though the bird calls in the early morning were pretty. Twenty eight persons sat, lay, or Lotus-sutraed in little groups around the natural grass bowl—forced to separate by city law prohibiting groups of twenty-five or more unless a permit is obtained. The "Oracle group," which was supposed to obtain the permit, did not come, and by eight A.M. Yogi Bhajan had not appeared.

The name of Yogi Bhajan's organization is "3HO— Healthy, Happy, Holy," and he has centers in "California, Texas, New Mexico, New York, Florida, Washington, D.C., Philadelphia, and New Jersey," (according to *The Post-Advocate*, Alhambra, California, January 27, 1970).

On a Wednesday evening in The Universalist Church, Swami Satchidananda led a service for about two hundred young people.

The Swami wore an orange nightgown . . . In front of the altar, he sat on a big chair, cross-legged, gazing down like a benign, amused father on his young American flock. Business certainly must be better here than in India, I thought.

The Swami seemed to me like our missionaries in his travels around the country. Swamiji (his nickname, though other Yogis are called it too) gives out ecstatic love and receives it in return from his countless young admirers. He probably writes home about the "natives," of America, how his faithful followers listen to him, laugh at his little jokes, and obey his urgings to be holy.

As the service was not consistently interesting, I looked around me. A young man in the front pew, Ravi, led us in a chant with his beautiful voice, "Haree . . . yom. Haree . . . yom." The young voices responded—all of those melodious tones coming from the beautiful young girls sitting cross-legged below the Swami (not *quite* all were beautiful).

Ravi was going on a bit long when the Swami cut in with his own "Har yee yom"—a deeper, more resonant, more manly but less beautiful voice. The Swami chanted, "Om—shanti—om." It was just like a return to childhood—happy, simple, rhythmic, and free.

I thought that this guy must be a sort of father to them—loving and foreign (very important as he is not identifiable with middle-class American Dads who are uninteresting or authoritarian). The Swami is the sort of father they all wish they had. I didn't think this Swamiji was particularly competent (in retrospect I disagree now with this judgment) but the time seemed ripe for Swamis, any Swamis. These kids were dying for something to believe in.

After the Swami's sermon there was a question period. A young man asked, "Hinduism is a philosophy of accepting the status quo. What should one do if a landlord turns off the heat or down South someone is killed?"

The Swami replied, "Hinduism is not fatalism. It is up to

your own free will. Some can do something about it. Those who cannot must accept it as the will of God."

When I left before the end of the service, an usher in a light brown business suit, standing by the desk in the rear, looked at me sadly. I was of the older generation who had lost this opportunity for truth. It was also a superior smile. I was too old and square to ever be able to appreciate the Swami.

Some days later I had an interview with him.

The Swami lives in an immaculate living-room-office, dining room, kitchen, and bedroom, served by a young secretary-cook, who is an American girl. Downstairs are three other apartments where twenty of his disciples, all young American men and women, live. The boys sleep on the floor—three to a room. The girls are in separate quarters. Hari, previously of the Bronx, New York, son of a house-painter, had long curly hair, was quick, gentle and efficient in showing me around. He is the co-head of the New York center along with Bhashkar—another Yoga disciple, under the Swami.

Swamiji does Yoga practice in the early morning, lectures and sees people most of the day, and eats one main meal at noon.

Despite his warm and saintly character, the Swami was stern in giving orders to his children. At the beginning he insisted I question his assistant before continuing our interview—"These questions are answered in our pamphlets" —although almost all of my questions could be answered only by him.

There are an exceptionally large number of pretty girls at the Integral Yoga Institute. Most of the disciples go out to work during the day. In the practice room were several men and girls in tortuous positions. "Usually each person contributes a dollar when they come for Yoga," said Hari, and my interview with Swami was later allowed to resume.

"Are you a father-figure in the psychological sense to your flock?" I said.

_ The Swami replied, "I am a father-figure to my children.

They see the materialism, the pollution in this very advanced country. Their parental relations have not been satisfactory. I give them the spiritual. These problems exist throughout most of the younger generation in America."

I said, "A young man the other night said that the Hindu philosophy supported the status quo and asked what one should do about landlords turning off the heat and the murders of Civil Rights workers in the South. You replied it was up to the individual's capacity. This, in my opinion, did not fully answer his question. What would *you* do in these situations or what would you advise *him* to do?"

"I would see the landlord and try to mediate a situation where there is clearly a strain."

"Did you come here because support for Yoga was declining in India? Or because you were having difficulties?"

"I did not leave Ceylon because interest in Yoga was declining. I have a successful Ashram there with thousands of followers. In Ceylon I am called on to settle labor disputes. Some of my American students, when they saw my beautiful small house on the river, a quiet place, were amazed when I left. But I go where I am asked."

"Did you ever think you would wind up in America?"

With a broad smile, he replied between the carefully rolled layers of his beard, "I accept where I am."

The Swami had come to America in 1966 at the urging of the artist, Peter Max, and with the financial assistance of Conrad Rooks, the millionaire who made the personal film about his years as a junkie called "Chappaqua."

LOS ANGELES

Most of the six girls and eight men were out putting up posters announcing Swamiji's lecture a week later. The Swami would soon fly out. When I arrived the three young women in the house at first thought I was a City inspector, as they were being forced to move because of the complaints of some neighbors over the extra parking and the use of the rented house for other than residential purposes.

One of the three girls in the house was pregnant. ("The pregnant girl came to the Institute pregnant. Yoga can never throw out or turn anybody away as undesirable," Swamiji wrote to me.) "We're all celibate now," they said.

Anne Asher, which is not her real name, had hazel eyes, long dark hair and a face that was oval and full-faced, even with a slight double chin. But her intensity and beauty grew on me. "I had a nude scene in this film. I'm the girl the hero marries in *Crash!* a teenage film, just before the police take him away as he has murdered his wife after taking LSD. That was at the beginning of the film.

"Most actors are heavy on sex. When they hug, they put their arms and everything in it, but I avoided it. The director after shooting every day would order vodka for everyone —'Have a drink.' I never would, though I would stay for the party.

"We meditate at six A.M., do asanas next, then eat breakfast, go to work, and clean the house."

THE LITERATURE OF YOGA

Bliss Divine by Sivananda, which was recommended to me by Hari of the Integral Yoga Institute in New York, says on sex:

". . . It is really shocking to hear the stories of some boys. Many college students have personally come to me and told their pitiable lives of gloom and depression, brought about by heavy loss of semen by unnatural means. . . . Lions, elephants, and other powerful animals have better self-control than men. . . . But it is an uphill climb to get rid of the sexual impulse. He who has completely eradicated lust and is established in mental celibacy is Brahman or God Himself . . .

"Repression or suppression of the sexual desire will not help very much. . . . If the sexual energy is transmuted into a spiritual energy by pure thought, it is called sex-sublimation in Western psychology.

"The Yogi gains control over the astral nature of semen and thereby prevents the formation of the very fluid.

"The body of a man who has this ability has the scent of a lotus. A man who is not celibate, in whom gross semen is formed, may, on the other hand, smell like a buck goat.

"Some ignorant people say, 'It is not right to check passion. We must not go against nature. Why has God created young, beautiful women?' . . . When they lose their property, wife, and children, when they suffer from an incurable disease, they will say: 'O God, relieve me from this horrible disease. Forgive me for my sins.' "

Christopher Isherwood, an important writer of the Thirties, regarded at the time on the same level as Orwell and Hemingway emigrated to Southern California and diminished fame. And then like Aldous Huxley, he turned inward, co-translating with commentary a certain Swami Prabhavananda's *How to Know God, The Yoga Aphorisms of Patanjali*. The first half of this book leads one to the familiar, if frequently inaccurate, conclusion that "getting religion" is inimical to the writer's art, though not his soul. There are many sweet nonentities of expression, an undertone of pessimism, but there is the virtue of clarity not typical of other Yoga writers. The second half of the book is more convinced and convincing, stylistically and religiously.

His pessimism: the individual reviewing his life after death—"Obviously for the vast majority of us, this experience cannot be other than bitterly humiliating and painful."

A beautiful quote from Swami Vivekananda: "After long searches here and there, in temples and in churches, in earths and in heavens, at last you come back, completing the circle from where you started, to your own soul and find that He, for whom you have been seeking all over the world, for whom you have been weeping and praying in churches and temples, on whom you were looking as the mystery of all mysteries shrouded in the clouds, is nearest of the near, is your own *Self*, the reality of your life, body and soul."

He explains that the sutra is as brief as possible because originally it was transmitted by memory in the days before there were books.

Raja Yoga by Swami Vivekananda, who "gave up his mortal body" in 1902, is a learned disquisition outlining the theology (*samadhi, samskaras, gunas,* etc.) and practice of this divine-seeking life. He offers also the following attractions on becoming a Yoga:

"He can make himself as minute as an atom or as huge as a mountain."

"He can hear sounds uttered miles away."

"Whenever he wishes, light flashes from his body."

"The yogi can enter a dead body and make it get up and move."

It should, however, be pointed out that these sensational powers are only a minor part of *Raja Yoga.*

CHAPTER XIII

Hare Krishna

Possibly the best known of America's new religions is the Hare Krishna movement. Their Indian costumes, shaved heads, and chanting in groups in public places in almost every big U.S. city have attracted television and press publicity. Millions of people have noticed them.

Lester Kinsolving in a column in the *Seattle Post-Intelligencer*, of June 7, 1970, contrasted "the International Society for Krishna Consciousness" to the Indian seer Krishna Venta in Southern California in the Fifties. Declaring himself "The Messiah," and enjoying considerable success, he finally tried to appropriate his followers' wives and was blown up by twenty sticks of dynamite set off by two enraged husbands. "Only the Messiah's false teeth survived the explosion," reported Kinsolving. Krishna Venta turned out to have a long police record, including "burglary" and "violation of the Mann Act."

Naturally, if one is not already skeptical, such a column raises questions about the sensationally successful organization, the International Society for Krishna Consciousness, led by Swami A. C. Bhaktivedanta. This writer's opinion is that the Hare Krishna movement and its Swami are legitimate.

An interesting argument took place between the Swami and Dr. J. F. Staal, Professor of Philosophy and of South

Asian Languages, University of California, Berkeley, over whether the *Bhagavad Gita* required chanting. Both men cite conflicting sources from ancient texts, the Swami finally asserting that one must accept the Judgment of the chief propagator of the chanting of Hare Krishna, Lord Caitanya, a fifteen-century Indian monk or reincarnation of Krishna (their God). The *Los Angeles Times* in the article that started up the debate said, "Staal . . . believes that the Krsna [Krishna] sect is an authentic Indian religion and that its adherents are sincere."

A current book, *The Bhagavad Gita* as it is translated by the Swami Bhaktivedanta, contains "appreciations by Allen Ginsberg, Thomas Merton, and Denise Levertov." There is no doubt but that the Swami is what he says he is. Certainly his disciples are genuine.

When I was in Los Angeles in 1970 the Swami would not see me on the grounds of having no free time because of his writing. One of his associates became angry at me over some aspects of an article of mine which appeared in *Mademoiselle* magazine describing Hare Krishna, in part.

A brief history of the Swami Bhaktivedanta is supplied by "Hayagrivadas," also known as Howard Wheeler, a lecturer in English at Ohio State, and an early follower of the Swami. Hayagrivadas remembers encountering the Swami in 1966, who was then seventy, ambling along a street of New York's lower East Side. The Swami had apparently arrived in the U.S. some months earlier and had been given shelter in a Yoga center. Hayagrivadas said, "Prabhupad [the Swami] was a businessman in India, had money, but could not bring any from India because of rupee restrictions. He has not been in contact with his wife for several years as is customary for a sannyasin, an order that renounces the world, and has not seen their children since then." At about that time a young admirer of the Swami had given him a month's rent on a storefront. The Swami had rejected the advice of other Yogis to Westernize himself a bit, and wore the saffron robe "and marked his forehead with telok." So here was the elderly man with no money wearing outlandish clothes obeying the order of his spiritual adviser of thirty years earlier to come and convert the West.

Whether the Swami knew it or not, before boarding the Scindia freighter from Calcutta to New York, the hippie movement was in full swing. The storefront led to classes, the classes to chanting, the chanting to Tompkins Square and Allen Ginsberg. Stories appeared in *The New York Times* and the *Village Voice* and the Swami's appeal can perhaps be deduced from a flyer written and distributed at that time by Hayagrivadas which began with "STAY HIGH FOREVER. No more Coming Down, Practice Krishna Consciousness . . . END ALL BRINGDOWNS! TURN-ON through music, dance, philosophy, science, religion, and prasadam [Spiritual food]."

The Swami's followers grew rapidly in number, joyfully accepting his strict rules, and it spread first to San Francisco and then on to nineteen other locations over the next four years. There are now about one thousand members, almost all full time. The main source of support was soliciting money in the street and the sale of their own incense and books and magazines. Hayagrivadas recently wrote me that the Society has now modified its street fund-raising technique by giving away the literature and incense sticks and asking for a donation. Some fifteen thousand to twenty thousand attended "an annual Rathayatra Festival" in San Francisco.

The Hare Krishna adherents are located at centers in New York, Los Angeles, San Francisco, Boston, Buffalo, Seattle, Honolulu, Santa Fe, Washington, D.C., and New Vrindaban, West Virginia—to name a few—besides those in Canada, England, Australia, and Japan.

Each young man has a shaved head, except for a pigtail, so that the "Lord Krishna can pull one into greater consciousness." The girls wear saris. They leave their centers, usually a house near a college campus, day and night to chant in groups and attract passers-by. It's a slightly way-out sensation to hear their American accents, and see their young American faces above their saffron robes.

The surface impact of Hare Krishna on American life

can be seen from an article in the *Seattle Post-Intelligencer* of June 6, 1970. Under the headline "Two Godbrothers Guilty of Noise," was the story of how two devotees of Hare Krishna were convicted of "violating a city anti-noise ordinance." A jeweler, Ben B. Benton, owner of Benton's Jewelry, had complained that the chanters annoyed and disturbed his business.

NEW YORK

At the center on the Lower East Side, I was present at an evening kirtan, or service. Before the ceremony, devotees gathered around me, whispering repeatedly and sibilantly, "Hare Krishna," a divine sound in itself. They fingered prayer beads in their right hand and had a "rosary" concealed in a soft white bag. White clay, flown in from India, was smeared on each forehead.

Once the kirtan began it was like a children's game as the devotees danced, swaying back and forth from one foot to the other, chanting a rhythmic and unintelligible—to me—Indian hymn. (Gargamuni das Brahmachary, secretary of the Los Angeles headquarters, said angrily to me of this phrase which had appeared previously in the *Mademoiselle* article, "Working for seventy-five years for money and not being able to take it with you is a children's game!") Two girls in sari-like costumes prostrated themselves on the Oriental carpet before the altar, beating long drums. I joined in. A black youngster jumped up and down. The ceremony was enlivened by what appeared to be the dousing of a holy candle. The device was accidentally knocked to the floor. Only a quick scramble prevented a fire.

In the kitchen we sat cross-legged on a bare tile floor for dinner. I had been told to remove my shoes. Gargamuni says this shows one has "respect for the Lord, because of the leather which is the hide of an animal." It was a hot night and there was a sickening smell of greasy nuts, warm milk, rice, and apricots. The raw nuts were fried in Ghee, which is clarified butter made by boiling sweet butter for twenty-four hours. The milk is natural from the cow and not made impure by refrigeration.

Afterward, Brahmananda Das Brahmachary (Das means "serving" and Brahmachary is "the first order of the spirits"), who was formerly a young American of New York City, a round-faced CCNY alumnus said, "We sleep on the floor. Our kirtans [it can also mean 'expedition'] of going out into the city have been getting later—until 1:00 A.M.—so we cannot follow the schedule as closely as good yogis should." And he added earnestly, "We have a rule against sex outside of marriage, are vegetarians, and do not permit drugs."

I also talked to Indira, a tiny eighteen-year-old New York Puerto Rican who was getting married in two days. Peering through large glasses, she said that Hare Krishna was the answer for her and that she and her future husband, a student at Ohio State, were looking forward to participating in the center in Columbus.

Guidance is from their Swami, Prabhupad (another of his names) Bhaktivedanta, who has appointed advanced pupils as leaders of the centers. When he departs his body a twelve man board of directors will conduct the Society.

Another American member, now Gadadhar Das Brahmachary, went to Jamaica High School and Queens College. "My mother," says Gadadhar, "often asks me: 'Why don't you become a doctor?'" Sometimes his parents come and visit him.

"At Queens I majored in two successive subjects, and then I dropped out. I just wasn't interested. I joined the Air Force when I was being drafted. Also I was a bit of a Peacenik and did not want to go to Vietnam and thought I could get electronics training." After two years he was discharged "because of a detached retina." He said he was in drugs for a while and tried other philosophies. Gradually he was achieving more self-control, though when he first joined Hare Krishna, he found the strict early morning rise difficult. Chanting out in the street, he concentrates on the holy sound, and says he does not feel odd. "People call us everything but it embarrasses me to say which particular words.

"In Boston a gang of motorcycle guys broke into our house at about 2 A.M. Our guys were sleeping, but one of us stabbed one of them seriously with a knife. They were the ones who got hurt."

A gentle person, he would like to get married but Hare Krishna will always come first in his life.

Asked why the religion has three times as many men as women, he said, "Men are more intelligent than women. Women give one a lot of nonsense."

NEW VRINDABAN, WEST VIRGINIA

I asked directions in the general store of three youngish farm types.

"Ya mean, them hippies?"

The entrance to New Vrindaban, which is near Limestone, a hamlet set among the green rolling hills eight miles from Wheeling, West Virginia, is a two-mile-long trail. It was a day after a heavy June storm and the path was rutted and wet, the water still sliding down the hillside to the creek, the trees and grasses still moist. It was about an hour's walk, twice crossing small fords, ascending to the farm, which turned out to be a community made up of a somewhat dilapidated main house, partly restored, a tiny Buckminster Fuller geodesic dome, a couple of A-frames, an outhouse, a tent, and one or two small dwellings. There were five cows. The horizon was misty from the rains of the night before despite the warm afternoon sun.

I found Hayagrivadas, who owns the farm and who is in charge of the community, reading one of his Divine Grace's manuscripts in the A-frame on top of the hill. "Why is it necessary to have Indian food and clothing?"

"One of the reasons is that we would not be able to chant and solicit on the streets of American cities if we were in ordinary clothes. Many of us formerly dressed like hippies. This way we clearly look like a religion."

"But when you are in your centers?"

"Obviously Indian food reminds one more of Krishna Consciousness than a hot dog."

"Is it really a rebellion against the American way of life?"

"That might be it partly. This is a very a-spiritual country. The main reason is that our spiritual master wishes it." He added, "I initially opposed this assumption of Indian customs."

"From his point of view," I said, "he is an Indian living his Indian way of life in America like an American living the American way of life in India."

"But we do not see it like that," he replied. "We see this dress as transcendental. It is not Indian dress in that sense. It is the dress of a Krishna devotee."

"The group in Columbus has just been arrested for the eighth time," he went on. "There are twenty to thirty of us at New Vrindaban. Only ten percent drop out after a year; thirty percent in the first month."

We walked outside, where I found a young devotee working on the A-frame. He had a thin face, slightly haunted, and dark close-shaved hair.

"Krishna is in every blade of grass. Human beings are the highest form of consciousness. Our aim in life is to transcend our bodies."

We walked down the hill to the main farmhouse. As I was going, he said, "If you live a life of Krishna Consciousness, Krishna says that when you leave your body, if you think of Him you will achieve bliss."

LOS ANGELES

The temple—an imitation of Greek in style with a stucco exterior—plus adjacent headquarters and dormitories cost two hundred and fifty thousand dollars. "Half-paid for," said Gargamuni Das Brahmadiary proudly.

"I also make marriages. We select the partners in advance," he said. "Tomorrow we are having several weddings of a Brahmachary and Brahmacharyni."

"What do you think about when praying?"

Pointing to a painting of a turbaned young man half-kneeling before another, both of whom were wearing classical Indian clothes, he said, "Arjuni is depressed. He does not want to fight the enemy, many of whom are relations. But Lord Krishna tells him to fight, that he must do it for Lord Krishna, that killing his own family members is liberating them from their bodies so that they are punished for their evil and will not suffer for it in their next incarnation."

"Do you mean that if you decided to kill me," I said, "that you would be liberating me?"

"No. That could only happen when Lord Krishna was present. The killing then was not killing at all because it liberated them from their bodies. He killed six hundred and forty million of them." This was Indian religious legend, apparently believed by the Hare Krishna members.

Before we went into the altar room for the weddings, a boy with a missing ear said, "I lost it in an accident ten years ago. Before joining Hare Krishna, I was a construction worker." My wife later said he needed warmth and love.

Gargamuni spoke in his speech of "illicit sex." One of the brides was dark-haired and pretty, another rather unattractive, a third plump and sweet-faced. The slightly older monk, who conducted most of the ceremonies, said into the microphone that they could never separate, and that they must raise their children in Krishna Consciousness. Haltingly he asked each couple "if they would help the other grow in Krishna Consciousness." Each girl was "to faithfully serve" her husband. The parents of one of the girls nodded assent when asked if they gave away their saffron-robed daughter. (Only one of the six pairs of parents was present for their children's wedding.) The couples placed garlands of flowers around each other's neck. Each groom put some paint on the middle hair-part of his bride and also a forehead mark.

Then the chanting began. The doors to the altar were

1. Espousing Transcendental Meditation, Maharishi Mahesh Yogi drew a crowd of over 2100 at Harvard's Sandere Theater. Actress Mia Farrow upper right.   UPI

2. In mystic ceremony, sorcerer and High Priest of the First Church of Satan, San Francisco, baptizes his daughter with a sword.   UPI

3. The young American youths with shaved heads, the girls in saris, leave their Hare Krishna centers day and night to chant in groups and attract passerby.

Duane Michals

4. Pir Vilayat Khan, the Persian Sufi Mystic, comes to America four times a year to counsel his followers who practice meditation, Dervish dancing and are vegetarians.

5. At the height of his fame, Elijah Muhammad appeared at the convention of his American followers (largely male) at the Chicago Coliseum in 1964.

UPI

6. The beachfront location, at Santa Monica, California, of the Japanese Buddhist sect which is the second largest of the new American religions.

7. Swami Satchidananda in front of the altar at the beautiful Universalist Church in New York gazes down on his young American flock like an amused benign father.

8. John Leiter, a college freshman, follower of the Indian mystic, Meher Baba, walks the shore of the 500 acre Meher Baba Spiritual Center at Myrtle Beach, S. Carolina.

closed, then opened. More and more made jumping motions. A tall young man waved his head back and forth and mumbled with an expressionless smile during the service earlier. Now he jumped up and down like a five-year-old before Krishna's altar, skin rashes showing under his gown. Two little girls walked around offering a candle over which devotees and spectators passed their hands and touched their foreheads. There were looks of ecstasy on many of the faces.

SEATTLE

The devotees were appealing a conviction for making noise. Some young people said, "The Hare Krishna kids are often getting arrested for blocking the sidewalks. Three or four out of seven nights they are picked up, and each time they come right back to the same place."

"His Divine Grace is a realized soul. In his presence there is a feeling of bliss. I have met him three times. Two of them were for my first and second initiations," said Gajendra Das Brahmachary, a tall thin youngster.

"Our worship is a little different here. We can vary from center to center. Our three altars are to Cartamaschee, Balarama, and Vyasasana."

The living room was converted into a pine-paneled and carpeted shrine. There were only six of them, though two Brahmacharynis had just arrived.

BOULDER, COLORADO

Five devotees had recently joined the local temple, a suburban house on which they were paying two hundred and fifty dollars a month rent. "There's not enough space for the eleven of us now and we're planning to move to Denver, where the rents are cheaper than the high ones in this university town."

"Dottie Dimple," as she called herself, said, with a pert smile, "We go into Denver every day for Sankirtan at 11:30

A.M., getting back at 7 P.M. Some strange people come up to us, calling us the 'anti-Christ,' and 'Communists,' particularly middle-aged women. Southern Baptists follow you arguing. You can't get away from them. It puts you into Maya, a detachment of the soul from the real self."

DENVER

In Denver they were chanting and speaking and passing out flowers in the plaza in front of the big department store located near the Hilton Hotel. One monk addressed a group of young men lounging nearby, "You think getting a new car will make you happy. But it will break down, need repairs, cost you money. What will you have? With Hare Krishna there is divine love." The bystanders stared at the young monk.

A policeman came up and told the monks to walk around the block.

A tall young man, dressed in blue jeans was chanting with them, swaying from one foot to the other. At times he stopped his chanting. All the while the little cymbals were crashing and the four Hare Krishna Brahmacharys had joyous looks on their faces. Three businessmen passed by, stopping to smile and question each other about this phenomenon.

The blue-jeaned youngster chanting with them said, as the others were picking up their red and white carnations and their drum to start marching again, "I went to the Temple in Los Angeles a couple of times. I ran away from home when I was fifteen. I was thrown out of my family's house in Denver a few days ago. My name's Michael. I'm nineteen."

"How do you stand with the draft?"

He shrugged his shoulders and smiled. "I don't know." His blue eyes narrowed suspiciously and he rocked cockily on the balls of his feet.

DETROIT

A year ago there were only a few members. Now there were twenty, although ten had just left for Chicago.

Narottamananda, the cook at the Detroit Temple, a short, friendly, charming young man, age about twenty, said, "His Divine Grace was told to come to America in 1936 by his spiritual master, Sri Srimad Bhakti Siddhanta Saraswati Goswami Maharaj, not long before he left his body.

"Prabhupad is seventy-four, but he looks younger every year. His skin becomes softer and his wrinkles are disappearing."

Narottamananda said he had been a junior at the State University in Buffalo until January, 1969, "and went there because there was nothing else to do. It is a bad society in which we live, and I didn't want to go to Vietnam." His younger brother is interested in Hare Krishna. His older brother "is in the materialism thing a physicist. My father, a college administrator, refused to visit the temple.

"You don't need buildings," he said cheerfully, waving vaguely in the direction of the slum section of blacks near Wayne State University where the Detroit Temple is located. "All you need is two acres and a cow."

A cop car drove by and he waved to it, crying happily, "Hare Krishna!"

Inside the house on the altar were large dolls colorfully attired. A large platter of food is offered to them, and then eaten by the devotees. Narottamananda continued, "A carpenter told the king not to enter the room without knocking. The king broke in, the carpenter fled, and left behind the half-finished carvings who were Lord Jaganath, which is another manifestation of Krishna. Krishna shows himself in wood, glass, minerals. We worship these wooden dolls and dress them up because we are human beings and need material objects to venerate, as we can not see Krishna."

Wearing a tiny saffron robe, a boy about six told me, "I live here. My father and mother don't love me. I haven't seen them in a year."

I had to leave for the airport. Narottamananda yelled to the same cops who happened to be passing by again.

"Hey, how do you get to the airport?"

As the police car pulled into the parking lot, the big cop behind the wheel gave Narottamananda a friendly grin. His partner smiled in a funny way.

THE LITERATURE OF YOGA

Kṛṣṇa Consciousness by A.C. Bhaktivedanta Swami calls itself "the topmost yoga system," and speaks on one of its fifty-seven pages to "my dear young girls and boys."

As an outsider, I should report that the author would probably categorize me as he does on page 49: "Those who are non-devotees . . . cannot explain the science of God."

Most of this little text, selling for fifty cents, featuring an ardent (presumably American) disciple on the cover, may have been delivered originally as a sermon. It outlines in a relatively lucid style with a complexity no greater than a Protestant pamphlet or Roman Catholic catechism the virtues of the Swami's sytem. "Lord Sri Krsna is that Supreme, the Personality of Godhead. I [in other words, humans] am pure soul." "False ego" occurs when "pure soul touches matter." We must liberate ourselves from "false ego" by chanting "Hare Krsna."

The Swami has strong views. Followers in relation to the guru should be like Arjuna, Krsna's first disciple: "Whatever You are saying I accept."

The Swami describes "transcendental ecstasies," as: "1. Being stopped as though dumb, 2. perspiration, 3. standing up of hairs on the body, 4. dislocation of voice, 5. trembling, 6. fading of the body, 7. crying in ecstasy, and 8. trance." Once I chanted for a brief while at a wedding ceremony, and noticed in myself the beginning of such symptoms—dizziness, happiness, the start of a sort of deep trance.

Less attractive than some of the above qualities is the Swami's evident intolerance of other forms of Yogi ". . . the bogus *yoga* system which is going on in the West these days. The *yoga* systems which have been introduced into the West by so-called *yogis* are not bona fide." He condemns in part the U. S. government: "Now we are training boys who are spiritually inclined, and they are unnecessarily being forced into military service." But he approves of a special class of "military men." Society must have its "brahmanas or it is a dead society." The rest of us—businessmen, writers, politicians—are compared to "asses, mules, and oxen" while "a race horse [devotee] is required for different purposes."

A similarly priced little book titled *Easy Journey to Other Planets* offers the unlimited wonders of the spiritual planetary ("Vaikuntha") system maintained by Krishna Himself.

The Swami opens with the ingenious comparison of the scientific discovery of "the anti-proton" which is thought to be anti-matter and "the real anti-matter" which is "spirit."

He states that the gross materialist may try to approach the anti-material worlds with spaceships, satellites, and rockets, which he throws into outer space, but with such means he cannot even approach the material planets in the higher regions of the material sky, to say nothing of those planets situated in the anti-material sky far beyond the material universe.

He warns that if one must enjoy material facilities, one should journey to planets in the "material" sky by utilizing yogic powers. He referred to the rocket ships as playthings of no use.

Though *Easy Journey* is at times roughly and repetitively written, it is believable (assuming one accepts as an initial premise the efficacy of prayer or magic or the other world), the following stretched my credibility: "Maharaj Bharata, despite a life of severe penances, thought of a stag at the time of his death and thus became a stag after death. However, he did retain a clear consciousness of his past life and realized his mistake."

Yet a third inspirational tract is written by A. C. Bhaktivedanta, *Krsna, The Reservoir of Pleasure and other essays.* It tackles the social scene in America head on. "It is not a very good condition, when the young generation, which is the future hope of the country, feels that there is no hope. Their future is dark. Why? Because they have no direction. What is the aim of life? What will they become? Their philosophy is work hard, get dollars, and enjoy as you like. This is misguidance . . . that cannot give total satisfaction." So the mysterious East triumphs again.

Superior to these pamphlets is one of the Swami Bhaktivedanta's several books, *The Teachings of Lord Chaitanya,* published by the society's own press, ISKCON. He has also written a new translation of *The Bhagavad Gita As It Is* and is now working on a sixty-volume "work of translation and elaborate commentary of the Srimad Bhagwatan." *The Teachings* carries on its back page recommendations from Allen Ginsberg, the late Thomas Merton, Professor Edward C. Dimrock of the University of Chicago, and the late Prime Minister of India, Shastri, among others. This learned blessed book contains many recitals of the same thoughts and devotions (similar to the endless chanting of Hare Krishna)—undoubtedly more stimulating to his followers than outsiders. Basically the book is a complex theological exposition of the thought of the founder of the order, Chaitanya Mahaprabhu, born in India on February 18, 1486, and who was regarded as an incarnation of Krishna.

There are also numerous attacks on the impersonalist Indian philosophers. There is emphasis on a class system, though follower of Krishna can come from any caste. And amidst India's poverty and disease in the fifteenth century there are descriptions of Chaitanya himself and some of his closest disciples acquiring wealth before turning to teaching.

Chaitanya was born amidst "loud cheers of Haribol" from bathers "in the Bgaghirathi." At the age of fourteen or fifteen he married Lakshmi Devi, who died in East Bengal, from "snakebite." He became a great holy man, was regarded as God, and defeated in argument several rival yogi who were converted by him.

Krishna or Chaitanya came in this age of "Kali Yuga," one of four such milleniums, each millenia a different color, this one being yellowish, corresponding to the saffron robes of Chaitanya and his successors. The different hues reminded me of the endless colors of the superior intelligences portrayed in the science-fiction film *2001*. Kali Yuga was a bad age, and Chaitanya came to save it by means of chanting Hare Krishna, presumably a simple method being necessary in a period of great iniquity.

Though Chaitanya was Krishna, he denies this. It is interesting to note that in one of the pamphlets, the Swami Bhaktivedanta lists himself in the same line of descent as Krishna and Chaitanya. Then on page 79 he writes, "An incarnation of the supreme Lord never declares Himself to be an incarnation. But His followers, with reference to the context of the authoritative Scriptures, must ascertain who is an incarnation and who is a pretender."

Chaitanya's attitude on worldly sex was, "We are shackled by iron chains which are beautiful women. Every male is bound up by sex life; and therefore, sex life should be controlled."

But on lust in the Spiritual World, he wrote that, "This Krishna is always engaged in the bushes of Vrindaban to enjoy lusty activities with Radharani . . . [Radharani is a female incarnation of Krishna and the leading Gopi.]

"The actual form of Radharani is just like a creeper embracing the tree of Krishna. The damsels of Vraja, the associates of Radharani, are just like the leaves and flowers of the creeper. . . . The hearts of the Gopis flutter like dry leaves on the trees and when the leaves fall down to Krishna's Lotus Feet, they can never rise up again from there."

CHAPTER XIV

Meher Baba

The most lovable of the U.S.'s new religions is Meher Baba. It is a classic example of the growth of this phenomenon. The founder, Merwan Sheriar Irani, born of Persian parents in Poona, India, in 1894, was influenced as a young man by Sufism. He said he was God, the latest reincarnation; his predecessors having been Zoroaster, Rama, Krishna, Buddha, Jesus, and Muhammad. His religion is a form of Bhakti Yoga.

In 1925 he took a vow of silence, never again spoke another word, communicated with an alphabet board, and in 1954 abandoned even the board for hand gestures which were understood only by his mandali, his closest disciples. Baba always said his silence was motivated by the fact that men had not listened to previous incarnations of himself, and that all that needed to be said had been said, and now it was time to act.

Among his early followers were two upper-class women —Mrs. Elizabeth Patterson, an American, and Princess Norina Matchabelli, of the perfume family. Mrs. Patterson, an insurance broker in New York, an unusual occupation for a woman in the Twenties and Thirties, "was one of the first women ambulance drivers for the Red Cross during the First World War." She was on the icebreaker Malygin, one of the Soviet expeditions to the Arctic coordinating with Byrd, and is in *Who's Who of American Women*.

There is a story that Baba on his first visit to the U.S. in 1931, enjoyed a sudden popularity in Hollywood where he was taken up by a number of movie stars. Everyone asked him repeatedly to speak. Time after time he said he would, and then when the dates came he would not. Finally his followers extracted from him a promise that he would talk on a certain day. The Hollywood Bowl was rented and filled for the occasion, the crowd expectant for his first word which was to be of immense value for the salvation of men. The Avatar appeared on stage, and said not a word. This caused a great decline in the number of enthusiasts. However, Mrs. Patterson denies that the event took place—"he canceled shortly beforehand."

In 1952 Baba was seriously injured—on another of his visits to America—in a car accident in Prague, Oklahoma. A follower said, "This brought about his flattened nose." Mrs. Patterson says, "Baba had told his disciples in India years before that he would have to shed blood on the American soil."

About five years ago the nucleus of elderly followers— such as Mrs. Patterson (the Princess died in 1957)—were surprised by the beginning of the influx of the young. For them, having labored for years for the cause of an obscure, bizarre Indian mystic, this development must have been indeed gratifying. The number of followers may now be about seven thousand. An interesting article, "Search for Love," by Margaret Shannon, August 24, 1969, in *The Atlanta Journal and Constitution Magazine*, says, "his followers in the United States may not number more than five thousand."

Among many of the Baba young people, notably those who have been on drugs, there is considerable opposition to marijuana, LSD, and other drugs, one of the more prominent Baba youths being both as strident and as active in his condemnation of the drug culture as he had been when he was in it. Though Baba himself—like other yogis—deplored drugs, he gives it little emphasis in those of his writings which I have read.

In 1969 Baba died near Ahmednagar, India. During his

lifetime as many as one hundred thousand people at a time had visited Baba for "Darshan" (similar to an audience with the Pope), and after his death a very large crowd attended another one, some flying to India from as far away as Australia, Europe, and the U.S. In America, since his death, the growth of his followers has increased faster than ever before.

Among the communities where there are reported to be Baba groups, are Boston; Schenectady, New York; New York City; Washington, D.C.; Hampton, Virginia; Chapel Hill, North Carolina; Greensboro, North Carolina; Myrtle Beach, South Carolina; Savannah, Georgia; Atlanta; Miami; Chicago; Minneapolis; Denver; Tucson, Arizona; Manhattan Beach (Los Angeles), Pasadena; Berkeley; Oakland and San Francisco. The two most important are Sufism Reoriented in San Francisco, which distributes the Baba books and pamphlets, and the Meher Spiritual Center, run by Mrs. Patterson together with a Board of Trustees in Myrtle Beach, South Carolina.

Two books, recommended particularly by Baba lovers, are *God Speaks* and the five-volume *Discourses*. The first is regarded as Baba's "classic later work." The second, less philosophical, contains much practical advice on subjects such as sex, birth control, non-violence and the relationship between the mind and the heart. In *God Speaks* the author nowhere asserts his divinity, but in Volume One of the *Discourses* he writes, "Many persons, for example, want to be convinced of my divinity in order to be able to love me."

God Speaks, divine or not, is an extraordinary work outlining the history of God and the universe, containing highly technical charts on the growth of the soul and levels of consciousness. To a Western theologian it contains many challenges.

Possibly the most novel is an analysis of "THE BEYOND THE BEYOND STATE OF GOD, THE FIRST URGE AND THE CYCLE OF EVOLUTION OF CONSCIOUSNESS." God, in the beginning, was the ORIGINAL UN-

BOUNDED ABSOLUTE VACUUM STATE OF GOD. God was infinite, therefore EVERYTHING.

EVERYTHING must include NOTHING, which is latent in the former. CONSCIOUSNESS ALSO EXISTS AS NOTHING. "Because God is EVERYTHING and the Infinite, the opposite of the EVERYTHING, which is the NOTHING, must be most finite." From this Baba says that the universe is finite, therefore nothing, therefore illusory, consequently what we live in is illusory. Also, as I understand it, God Himself is struggling to achieve real consciousness of Himself in the evolution of the Universe. God might in a sense have been said to be asleep in HIS original state.

In the introduction to *God Speaks* by Don E. Stevens, he refers to a "meeting of the hierarchy atop a mountain in the Swiss Alps. A violent storm raged as Baba stood untouched in a shaft of light which pierced the disgorging clouds. Those who attended him were drenched as they stood waiting a few feet down the slope."

In *Discourses* Baba gave his views on sex which are similar to those of St. Paul's. Baba wrote: "Hence for the aspirant a life of strict celibacy is preferable to married life . . . For ordinary persons, married life is undoubtedly advisable unless they have a special aptitude for celibacy." . . . "Though humane and rational considerations demand and justify all serious attempts to regulate the birth of children, the use of physical means for securing this purpose remains fundamentally indefensible and unjustifiable . . . From the spiritual point of view birth control must essentially be effected through mental control and nothing else."

He writes, "Therefore lust is experienced as being HEAVY and love is experienced as being LIGHT . . . Thus in lust there is the accentuation of separateness and suffering, but in love there is the FEELING OF UNITY AND JOY."

Baba on the heart and mind:

"In the life of most persons the mind and the heart are at loggerheads and the conflict between the two creates confusion. The heart, which in its own way, feels the unity of life, wants to fulfill itself through a life of love, sacrifice, and service. It is keen about giving instead of taking . . . It does not care for the proofs or intellectual corroborations which the mind seeks while dealing with material objects. In its objective handling of the material world, mind is saturated with experiences of multiplicity and separateness, and therefore it feeds the egocentric tendencies which divide man from man and make him selfish and possessive . . .

"LOVE AND HAPPINESS ARE THE ONLY IMPORTANT THINGS IN LIFE, AND THEY ARE BOTH ABSENT IN THE DRY AND FACTUAL KNOWLEDGE WHICH IS ACCESSIBLE TO THE INTELLECT . . .

"The hidden depths of the ocean of life can be gauged only by sounding the heart . . .

"When there is such harmony the mind does not dictate the ends of life, but only helps to realize those ends which are given by the heart . . . In other words IT SURRENDERS ITS ROLE OF JUDGE, which it is accustomed to play in its intellectual queries concerning the nature of the universe, and accepts unquestioningly the dictates of the heart . . .

"The mind is the treasure house of learning but the heart is the treasure house of spiritual wisdom. The so-called conflict between religion and science arises only when there is no appreciation of the relative importance of these two types of knowledge . . .

"The mind has a place in practical life, but its role begins after the heart has had its say . . .

"Such harmony of mind and heart is the most important condition of the integral undivided life of spiritual understanding."

NEW YORK CITY

At a Baba meeting at 8 P.M. in a New York office, the Baba fans hugged, giggled, and laughed, said "Jai Baba," and sang a hymn to Baba called an "Arti" with the following chorus:

Consumed is my mind in your fire and flame:
  Accept it, O Meher, in Oneness.
Consumed is my heart in the sound of your name:
  Accept, O Meher, my Arti. Accept, O Meher, my song.

A wild ending included rhythmic foot-stamping.

A 1968 Dartmouth graduate, James Stephens, an easy-going, personable young man, said, "Initially, I greeted their assertion that Meher Baba was God with cynicism. 'So what?' I said. 'So was Father Divine.' For the fun of it I gave one of their cards to a girl on a New York City subway. By chance, she was a Meher disciple. All I can say is, my heart was touched. I can't explain why, but I believed. I only knew her for twenty-four hours. She gave me an introduction to her friends at the University of North Carolina. There are forty or fifty young people at UNC, mostly ex-hippies, who had been on drugs. A Baba follower lectured there and instantly thirty converted.

"When I visited them for a week, it was brotherhood. Meeting the older followers at the Baba Center in Myrtle Beach, South Carolina [Baba stayed there on three trips to the U.S], was, I imagine, like the feeling the early Christians had when Peter and Paul went around saying Christ was here and used this object."

Mr. Winterfelt, superintendent of a large building in New York City, and his wife are childless. Long-time devotees of Meher, they obviously love having their living room filled with young kids. The place was filled with reliquaries and pictures of Baba.

At the Winterfelt apartment, Dr. Allan Cohen, an assistant professor at John F. Kennedy University, Martinez, California, and one of the Harvard graduate students who worked with Leary and Alpert on psychedelic drugs, said he learned of Meher at a lecture he went to with Timothy Leary a few years ago, "Darwin Shaw, who was giving the lecture, was an Establishment type—stuffily dressed—and we weren't in that bag then, but watching on film Baba's reactions to his followers passing by him at a Darshan I could see he was alert and getting through to each of them."

ACROSS THE OHIO

At a Middle-Western university the president of the student body, Ken Atwood, and three of his friends discussed Baba:

Ken Atwood: "Have you seen Peter Townsend's new record? *Tommy's* based on Baba's discourses (the folk opera by *The Who*). This is Melanie's album with her Baba love. One of the lines is 'Meher Baba Lives Again.' This suits Baba because it's soft and quiet. I don't know who Melanie is, but this record is sold out in Florida. Three girls from Naples I met when speaking at University of Miami—the father of one of them designed the cover.

"I have been to several universities to speak of Baba, but only when I'm asked to do I speak to theology schools and church groups.

"Everyone at this university knows about Baba because there've been so many articles."

He continued—"We put Baba's picture here," pointing to wood-paneled lounge. "We sit in a circle, some on the floor or on chairs. There's no formal way . . . There are moments of silence . . . there is reading of Baba's words . . . We like to sing . . ."

His three companions, Mark, Patrick, and Douglas echoed —"We try."

Ken: "We sing Baba's songs. We sing Baba Bagawan. We have one of our own, which our friend Jane wrote—'Don't worry be happy, Meher Baba loves us all, illusions are many, but underneath them all, there's one reality, where you and I are one and God is love, and love is God and God and Man are One.'

"Usually the little children sing it and we try to follow them."

Mark: "We made up the tune."

Ken: "We sing it sort of sing-song. Jane composed it driving from Detroit.

"There was a conference on the Spiritual Unity of All Nations, in Detroit during September of 1969. I talked about . . . the spiritual change among young people. I think Baba's love was there. There were mainly spiritual groups including Baha"i'."

Mark: "Usually some of Baba's words are read—his discourses."

Ken: "Often we have the Master's Prayer which Baba dictated. Once in a while people give their own experience. Sometimes we'll have a film or a tape.

"Be sure to meet Dave Michaels in Los Angeles. He's a character—big handlebar mustache. He was one of the last Westerners to meet Baba. Baba called him his Muckawallah —not wali, that's an advanced soul, I don't want to confuse it—worker, a term of endearment, also means his mustache."

Douglas: "It might sound far out. I want to make Baba my life, if one can incorporate into oneself what one already is since Baba says we already are God."

Mark: "My experience has been through the heart more than the intellect, more of an experience, with the other Baba followers sharing the love with them and for Baba."

Douglas: "Most of our friends are in Baba."

Ken: "There's something of Baba in everyone. Unless you can share Baba, it's difficult but not impossible. Most of my closest friends are Baba. We come from such different backgrounds, Baba holds us together—we have some kids in the group, a secretary, a lawyer, a man who works at a laboratory, and a technician. The technician is black. We have people from the hip district. We had some black ladies who started to come to our meetings, but they work late hours so they had to drop out. They were out of work at the time. They were domestics."

Patrick: "We have a white eighty-six-year-old lady. She was here and saw a black and was a little upset. A month afterward she was somewhat upset with black children when we had a party for them. Now she wants a picture of herself and the black children."

Ken: "My girl friend's a Baba lover."

Douglas: "I date Ken's sister who loves Baba."

Patrick: "None of us were in drugs. The week before I met Baba I was contemplating my first joint."

Ken and Douglas: "We find his teaching on sex easy to live with."

Ken: "Baba says celibacy and marriage are the two alternatives for the serious aspirant. I'm sure some of the students here have had sexual experiences, including some Baba followers. There are no set rules on this. Baba treats each person as an individual. Baba never does things through coercion, only through love. You give up your desires voluntarily for the sake of love."

Mark: "If we slip, we don't feel guilty. If we succeed or fail he told us not linger or to worry, but to learn from the experience."

Patrick: "We fail every day—in other things."

Douglas: "When we slip, we understand that we really don't understand."

Ken: "There is a sexual revolution going on. Baba meant marriage as a joining together of two human souls for their mutual development, but not necessarily appearing before an altar. This is the highest type of marriage. This attitude is shared by young people all over. Spiritual understanding frees us. We have trouble only when we don't have spiritual understanding.

"I think with the new dawn of understanding there will be different traditions developing. The most important thing is Baba wants us to fully become what is in us, to be natural."

Patrick: "On the subject of the draft, Baba says first to have a spirit of flexibility. You may do one of several things, such as C.O., or perhaps seminary. Perhaps I'll get a job or I'll fail my physical. Whatever one does, accept it and do your best. If one is drafted, do the best you can. It's not what we do but how we do it."

Ken: "Sex is a strange question."

Ken, Douglas, Patrick, Mark: "We sometimes sing 'Punchinella' which we learned from the children. We also do the Baba Machine where each person imitates a

different sound of the machine—squeaks, movements, clicks
—until it explodes."

All of the Baba follower's bedrooms had photos or paintings of the Avatar. One was against the wall beside a lower
bunk-bed. "Baba says if you say 'Jai Baba' on waking up
and going to sleep, you'll be happy for the day," said
Charles, a golden-blond, curly-haired twenty-year-old. They
press palms together saying "Jai Baba" when greeting each
other on campus. The bedrooms were in varying states of
disorder.

These four young men were of the mainstream student
body and were not the hippie-artistic-intellectual-SDS types.

Note: The above names have been changed and the location of the university not given.

DENVER

On walking round the house, having had no answer to
my rings, I asked a woman watering the lawn across the
street if anyone was in. "You never know who's living
there," she said with a wry smile.

Roughly two years ago, Dave Michaels, reputedly a
friend of Timothy Leary's, who was visiting Denver, spoke
about Meher Baba on KTLN's night show. Listening were
Frank and Anne Sawyer. They wrote to Sufism Reoriented
to get literature from them. Working for his B.A. in Eastern Philosophy at Metropolitan State College in Denver,
Frank works during the day as a chef at The Crab Apple
Orchard, a local restaurant. They have three small children. Anne, his wife, is a pretty lissome girl who was a
Roman Catholic. They live in a big rambling decaying-
paint wooden house in a tree-lined, green-lawned section of
a Denver suburb, where the other homes, which are often
brick, are as neat and manicured as the Sawyer's residence is
not.

"We advertised in the local underground paper, *Chinook*

(ironically named for a type of helicopter in Vietnam) about holding a Baba meeting," says Anne.

"There are about two hundred Baba lovers in the Denver-Boulder area," Frank told me over the phone from the restaurant. "Last Sunday fifty-one came to the meeting."

The growth of Baba resulted in their moving from a small one-bedroom apartment to their present rented house —one hundred dollars a month.

Also living with them is Rocco Conte and his "chick." Rocco is ex-drug scene, a Vietnam veteran, curly-haired, and also Baba lover.

The house is filled with photos of the Avatar.

Sitting in the kitchen that afternoon was fifteen-year-old Melinda Ryder, wearing the traditional long hair, an attractive roundish-faced girl, who lives down the street from the Sawyer's: "Sometimes my parents call me crazy for believing in Baba when they're deliberately trying to hurt me. At other times they're sympathetic. I go to a Catholic High School.

"A bunch of us kids were sitting around one evening when we first saw all these long-hairs going up to this house. 'Wow!' we thought. What's going on here! I was curious."

Anne remarked, "We've had some difficulty convincing the neighbors that orgies do not take place here."

Anne said, "Our six-year-old son is often ridiculed by the other children in school because of Baba. They call Baba dirty words. He is torn between Baba and the straight culture and Christian religions of the other children, but we feel it gives him a choice."

Anne Sawyer, Rocco Conte, and Melinda reported that there were also followers of Anthony Brooks's Universal Link—a belief in astral projection, Paramahansa Yogananda, Theosophy, meditation groups, readers of the *Bagavad Gita*, and disciples of Nichiren Shosu in the Denver area.

Note: The above names have been changed.

MYRTLE BEACH, SOUTH CAROLINA

The green gate beside the sign *Meher Spiritual Center* at the edge of the deep green forest was padlocked. A quick phone call bearing the name of a Baba lover will lead to a welcome at the brick house concealed amidst the upper-income residential estate. Briarcliff Acres—the home of Mrs. Elizabeth Patterson—who despite her reluctance to admit it, is the main benefactress of the retreat. Alongside of Mrs. Patterson's comfortable, unpretentious residence is a five-hundred-acre tract of land bordering on a mile-and-a-quarter of beach and whitish sand dunes. There is also an inner strip of seashore undergrowth before the forest begins. Here are the sacred buildings of the Avatar, who "dropped his body" on January 10, 1969.

In immaculate condition is a library of white-painted pinewood containing Baba's books and the works of other saints such as Teresa of Avila and St. Francis of Assisi. A cluster of dark pine cabins is located in a circle, near enough to the main house so "Baba's hand-claps could be heard." Baba's car, a 1958 blue Ford sedan, up on cinder-blocks, is still shiny. There is a sign in front of it. A large meeting hall which Baba used for audiences of two or three hundred people and two chairs where he once sat are now roped off (they were being worn out from too many Baba-lovers sitting in them). And then Baba's house, *his house*, a red-brick bungalow of about six rooms, fully furnished. He visited the center three times, the last in 1958. The longest period he spent there was three months. In one room were reliquaries under a plastic top—his robe, white underpants, a lock of hair—gray from his old age, a black lock from younger years, and another, deep brown, as a young man. There is an alphabet board by which he had communicated, and nearby, the pillow with the bloodstain where his head rested after the automobile accident in Prague, Oklahoma, 1952.

Deer roam the forest. Here are Spanish moss, high pines,

oak, and myrtle. Jackdaws and whippoorwills cry as the wind rustles through the verdure and on over the mile-long lake which is bordered with rushes. The lake—a fresh-water body near the sea—also contains a nine-foot long alligator. "Baba ordered that the center be where there was fresh water, virgin land, neither too hot in the summer for Northern followers or too cold in the winter for Southern ones."

The atmosphere of love, of conviction, and of non-visual light shining from the faces of the three women was similar to that of the nuns in Catholic convents. Who were they?

One was Mrs. Patterson, an elderly lady whose white hair was covered with a white net sprinkled with tiny pearls. Heavily stooped on one side, she had a clear glass necklace linked by a silver chain signifying Baba's observation that "I am the chain which brings the true religions of the world together." She presided quietly at the head of the dining-room table. "I liked to travel. My husband respected this, which was one of the reasons I married him . . . The first time I saw Baba, I knew I had known him before, so familiar was his face . . . The purity of his character was like that I have seen in nature."

Seated opposite me was Kitty Davy, a great niece of Florence Nightingale's, an energetic and compactly-built Englishwoman. Her gray hair was pulled back behind a lined healthy face whose weathered skin mirrored twenty years in India where she had served as Baba's housekeeper. She spoke with the authority of a close disciple, and there were overtones of a Victorian upbringing in her clarion voice: "Baba says to be cheerful, not to worry."

"To be concerned," said the third woman.

"But not to worry. Inner control."

Mrs. Haynes, the third woman, had high cheekbones, delicate skin, and gray-blue eyes beneath grayish-black eyebrows. She had an expression of innocence like that of a young girl, or of an Alice in Wonderland, confronting a world where much was dismaying. She blinked a lot. Her lips were painted a soft red. She talked almost continuously in a voice that was a combination of a Southern accent and classical New York theatre. It was a steely-pure voice, like a rippling trout stream. Her nose was straight with a slight upturn at the end of it.

She took me on a tour of the center. Suddenly, half-jumping at a young male visitor in the kitchen of a cabin, where the young people can bring their own food and cook, she said emphatically to him, "You're always making biscuits."

She told me, "Mrs. Patterson is the head. Kitty is her assistant and Baba said I was to be the helper.

"Two to three thousand people, mostly young, visit every year. On weekends we'll have fifty-five or sixty. I have to ask them if they have any drugs." Mrs. Haynes said the men and women sleep in separate cabins. "Only once—a man we knew who was a friend and a beautiful girl he was serious about—did we have to tell them that he couldn't be in Cabin B."

Occasionally a young person moved along the car-wide trails. "The reason the trails have so many curves in them," said Mrs. Haynes, "is that Elizabeth did not want any big trees cut down."

We chatted with a young man with a stubby nose and curly red hair, whose last name was "Portnoy." "He works three days a week inserting newspapers in order to support himself living near the center. No one who works can live at the center," had said Elizabeth. "It is a place of retreat, for refreshment of the Spirit, to come to from time to time."

Mrs. Haynes said, "I played Blanche in the national company of *A Streetcar Named Desire*. Baba showed me the theatre was not for me. John Kerr had signed me for a starring role in a play and then gave the part to Glynis Johns. When I received the telegram telling me this, it took me ten minutes to understand what Baba meant when He said, 'The deeper role in life, for such as you, came about through many difficulties.'

"Once I was present with Him, and the sweat was pouring down His face. He was in pain. For once I thought of Him instead of myself. He looked at me and I heard—and this was the only time it ever happened to me, His voice was neither masculine or feminine—his inner voice said to me, 'I love you.' "

Baba—like other mystics—said he could move onto other levels of consciousness.

"Another time there was a difference between Elizabeth and me over who would read to him. He asked me to read out loud from Gibran's passage on Mary Magdalen before his mandali. I read and saw his fingers moving up and down quickly. I thought he was bored, but was told later he was thinking on another plane. I was calm in reading, which I never am in acting when I am in steely control.

"Being in beloved Baba's Presence was to be in the presence of pure Love. One felt . . . experienced . . . this purity of Love. There was a radiance of countenance that no words can express. Compassion . . . true compassion . . . flowed from Baba's eyes. I knew . . . experienced . . . that He had always known me . . . many, many times . . . and I, Him. The sweetness of expression was unbelievable. The embrace was not a physical touch. It was being enveloped in a warmth of great joy . . . peace . . . I remember especially how my mind was stilled . . . completely. All time seemed suspended . . . indeed during the entire stay. I saw only a glimpse of Baba's suffering. Though His smile was tender, and very beautiful, and happy, there was an underlying sadness that I felt or saw in His eyes. Baba's Love enveloped me in a very deep inward way. I felt, or knew, or experienced, that God loves me. I had always hoped so, but I did not believe it. When I was in Baba's Presence, I knew it. Baba knows my false self . . . knows all my terrible weaknesses . . . all . . . yet when He turned His glance upon me, He seemed to see only my *true* self . . . purity and love. For that is why He came . . . why He suffered . . . to help each of us to awaken this true self . . . to put it to work in our lives . . . to start our journey home to God."

PART III

Avant-Garde
Christian
and Jew

CHAPTER XV

The Process Church

The young members of The Process Church of the Final Knowledge love Satan, because Christ advised loving one's enemy. They will not talk to the press, though I was allowed to attend their services "as a member of the public." About two hundred members are situated around centers located in Boston and Chicago. They wear dark space-suits with red Satanic emblems sewn on the chests and are usu ally accompanied by German-Shepherd dogs.

The short pamphlet, *SO BE IT*, gives a few clues as to life in The Process. The anonymous author, evidently in his late twenties, was experienced in drugs, peace marches, "free sex," theosophy and psychiatry before joining The Process at the age of twenty-five. He learned about "unity with superhuman Beings" from a group in New Orleans. At that time there were about ten "Inside Processeans" who came from a full spectrum of economic, racial, and religious backgrounds—Arabs, Jews, Germans, near-illiterates and University graduates, panhandlers, and electricians. He was received into the Church "as an Acolyte" and a week later he became "an Initiate." Six weeks afterward he was baptized "with my new Process name." He says, "This is the fastest that these steps can be taken."

At the time, the entire group met in a three-story building in the "French Quarter of New Orleans. . . . But word had come down through the hierarchy that we should move; word from the Super Beings." Opposition from a few "nutters" who had misunderstood the Satan aspects was apparently not the reason. Some refused to go, preferring their "well-paid jobs, professional reputation, or beautiful homes." The rest moved to San Francisco where they organized a new chapter. In the next two years the author of *SO BE IT* also belonged to Process groups in Los Angeles, New York, Holland, France, Germany, Italy, and England," where he wrote his book.

When my wife visited the Cambridge chapter in Massachusetts, she wrote: "Fairly attractive house in Cambridge with three floors and a cellar. Everything is spotlessly clean. Besides a coffee shop, the cellar has a kitchen completed by the members, as well as a small workshop where some of them make handcrafted silver earrings, beads, necklaces, and rings. All lovely and I was very tempted to buy some.

"Sister Hogan greeted us as we came in with a very friendly welcome. Was polite and conscientious in answering my questions. After giving a tour of the cellar she told us a little about her Church.

" 'We worship Satan, Christ, and Lucifer"—she pointed to the silver pin with Satan depicted on it and to the cross representing Christ on her dress. 'We do not discriminate, one may say—that is the key.'

" 'We make our own bread. We live on the money the coffee shop brings in, on the literature we sell, and on donations.

" 'The main thing we try to achieve,' Sister Hogan said, 'is to be aware of the needs of others and to respond to them, no matter who those others are.' "

On a Saturday evening in Cambridge three months later a young man with blond hair came up to me in a khaki outfit looking like a mixture between a cowboy costume and a soldier's uniform. "Can you give me anything so I can attend The Process this evening?" I gave him a quarter.

As he walked down Inman Street looking for more

donors, I called after him, "Are you a member of The Process?"

"No," he said enthusiastically, a slightly wild expression on his handsome face, "but I'm hoping to join. It costs some four dollars for the activities."

I followed him to the meeting place and found, just outside the hall opposite the bulletin board, a large photo of "Robert De Grimston," who is reputedly the founder of the Process, with the long hair of Christ and an intense, slightly strange look in his penetrating eyes. The coffee shop had benches, wooden tables, and little lights with red shades. On the wall were murals in reds, whites, and gold, depicting a large dragon and an angel and several childlike figures.

Among the literature on a mantlepiece was a sort of sensitivity game, in which the object was that the "soul" and "body" apparently had to reach the final square of fusion between Christ and Satan. One of the squares required telling "what you are most ashamed of."

We trooped upstairs. Appearing occasionally were the German-Shepherd dogs. Suddenly I found myself in a room where sitting cross-legged in an oval, their backs to the walls, were about thirty young people. To my left was an attractive slim girl with dishwater blonde hair and squarish delicate features. To my right was a plump girl, her brown hair in a bun. Those present were a mixture of Processeans in their space-suits, others in casual clothes. Presumably many of the latter wearing crosses were novices. It was hot in the room. The girl obviously in charge had long black hair, her long sensitive face resembling a Joan of Arc.

"For our next meditation," she said in clear tones, her accent American but slightly clipped, "we will meditate on fear," and they all closed their eyes.

After about five minutes we heard her voice: "Bring yourself out of meditation gradually . . . you may now open your eyes."

Those present spoke of loneliness, inability to communicate, fear of the world, and of themselves. The girl on my

right remarked, "Fear is like a yellowish-brownish sub-
stance in the air. There has never, I think, been a conscious
moment of my life when it has not been with me."

A man opposite, who looked about thirty, read a poem
about the empty room within him. "Will I never escape
from it? Would no one ever enter it?"

The woman in charge said, "We will now do psychome-
try. We will split into pairs. You give your partner an object that has been on your person a long time and he will
close his eyes and holding it against his forehead, tell you
what he sees. If you do not have an object, give your hand
but it must be the hand which you use less. If you are left-
handed, give your right hand. We will then alternate."

She assigned us into pairs. To me she said, "You and
Sherrill." This turned out to be the girl on my left. I gave
Sherrill my wristwatch.

"How long have you worn it?" said Sherrill.

"Eight years."

"That's fine."

She closed her eyes, pressing my timepiece to her forehead. She was wearing a medium-blue matching top and
trousers with horizontal white stripes. Before she closed her
eyes I noticed they were blue and rather suspicious; she had
a slightly wide mouth. Her complexion was smooth and
white. The cross swinging from her neck cast a shadow over
her lap.

She spoke for about five minutes. "I see a mine under
water . . ."

"Do you mean a mine that one digs or a mine that explodes?" I asked.

"Like a time bomb . . . I see a trident. What does that
mean?"

"It was a sexual image," I replied.

"I see rushes on the water . . . I see a movie camera."

At one point a young male Processean with flowing black
hair crouched beside us and peered intently.

The girl in charge asked each of us, "How did it go?"

Sherrill said, "It was slow but it came through okay."

I said, "Most of what she said could have been interpreted in any way but some of it was accurate."

We then switched. She gave me her right hand. I gave my observations, eyes closed, reporting on the images that came into my mind.

She told the leader excitedly, "It was good. It really flowed."

I said, "I feel intense, slightly exhausted, and pleasant."

We had another meditation. Our leader said, "So Be It." She left the room.

After a coke in the coffee bar some of us returned to the meditation room. One girl in black had a lute, and beside her was a lovely girl—also in black—whose profile was innocent and pure. She had natural blonde hair and a creamy complexion. The lute-playing was beautiful—clear, lyrical, and youthful. Then playing a guitar she led us in chants, "Dadum . . . Lada-de-da . . . Dum . . . Dalada." We repeated each meaningless phrase after her and the room filled with soprano and lower tones. There were several readings by various Processcans on Lucifer, Christ, Jehovah, and Satan, and a discussion on the meaning of "Fire, Earth, Air, and Water." We shouted the names of Satan, Lucifer, Jehovah, and Christ. After each one we clapped our hands. At one stage there was organized but wild shouting, the beating of a drum, and "Sister Julia," a sweet shy girl, urged me to shake a "mariachi," which I did.

When we trooped out, one of the regular members came up to the young man to whom I had given the quarter.

"Are you all right?"

He nodded his head enthusiastically. During the service, he had seemed to be in a state of ecstasy that would break at any time.

Sister Julia told me how happy she was in The Process. "When I first saw them in London four years before, they frightened me." She said her father was Tahitian with some "American blood" and her mother was a Canadian. Julia's features were completely Caucasian. She had a small chin and a nice complexion.

Later, at the midnight meditation, four candles were lit on a glass-covered coffee table. About forty people filled the humid room. The woman who had led our telepathy session, now sitting at the top of the oval of worshippers said sharply, "We will meditate on materialism."

Later she said, "We will meditate on spiritualism."

If A Man Asks, recorded by Robert DeGrimston, sixty-seven pages long, written in April, 1968, is published by The Process Church of the Final Judgment, Balfour Place, Mayfair, London, England, W.1. The author makes frequent use of the rhetorical style with parallel sentences and repetitive rhythm, like a Presidential candidate delivering his acceptance speech. "Not a church or a group of human beings or a philosophy," The Process covers all time, according to the text, but we are now reading the end of it. People have the choice of joining the Process immediately, or of vacillating (which becomes "harder and harder"), or opposing it. "The third way is to die." At the Final Judgment those in the third category will see what they have missed: "Like Tantalus you shall see and know and feel without the power to partake. And that shall be your fate for all eternity." To support this harsh view of life, there are a number of Christ's grimmer quotations from the New Testament.

Those who come to The Process are accorded its benefits: "And we shall take them in and strip off them the agonizing shackles of mental conflict, and clothe them in Spirit of immortality." A person must face the existence of hate and love in his psyche.

The Process interprets "Blessed are the meek, for they shall inherit the earth" not as "the weak and weeping" but instead as "The few who accept what is . . . The few who give without counting the cost . . . Because they are basically strong, they do not *have* to make a superficial show of strength."

The book concludes with the explanation that its members wear black "as a symbol of the death of the world." The red insignia represents "the blood that man has shed among his fellow men." Silver, presumably the cross they wear, represents "the light of the New Beginning." When the Judgment is complete "White shall we wear for the end of the suffering, for the end of pain of countless millions of innocent creatures, whom man has subjugated and degraded, but whom God shall rise up, and glorify."

CHAPTER XVI

The Association for Research and Enlightenment A.R.E.

The Association for Research and Enlightenment, better known as "A.R.E.," is Christian, avant-garde, technically not a religion and in a sense, scientific. Its membership is not limited to followers of Jesus Christ and they have been known to sponsor a non-Christian speaker. A.R.E. officials say that it is not a religion, but readers can draw their own conclusions. It is based largely on the stenographic record of what Edgar Cayce said while in a sleeplike trance. Cayce's skill as a diagnostician and consultant of his clients' medical ailments is undeniable. Before his death at Virginia Beach, Virginia, in 1945, he had diagnosed the health of thousands. These comprised over half of his four thousand "readings," or trances. The others concerned Christianity, philosophy, reincarnation, the future, the past, and politics —virtually the entire range of human activity—both in this world and the next.

A.R.E.'s members often belong to "Search for God" groups—a blend of group therapy and early communal-type Christianity, although property is not shared. Mediums are not allowed to practice their alleged ability of contacting the dead at the "Search for God", sessions. Medical and archeological passages among the fourteen million transcribed words are still used by the members and others for guidance and research.

A higher degree of self-awareness is emphasized by the Edgar Cayce groups. The thirteen thousand members of the Association meditate silently in groups, talk about their dreams, and pray aloud for friends.

NEW YORK

Sally Baldwin, a free-lance editor in her twenties who lives in Manhattan, a graduate of Hofstra, Long Island, with an M.A. from Columbia, sat after a meeting in the yoga knees-legs-crossed position. She is disenchanted with organized religions because she thinks them externally rather than internally oriented, and too preoccupied with social commitments. In A.R.E., she believes she has discovered the supreme spirit; how mind, body, and spirit are one, and how the glands in her body are connected with the spirit and have a spirit life of their own. She had come to A.R.E. six months earlier "after undergoing a personal crisis, and I have learned it was all for the best. Now if I encounter a stumbling block, I can grow from the experience."

At the prayer meeting led by the New York director, Shane Miller, everyone recited the Lord's Prayer and chanted the names of those they wished help for, after turning out the lights. Sally sat motionless in a chair for ten minutes in the darkened room during the silent meditation, feet firmly planted on the ground, palms turned upward in her lap, and tried to think loving thoughts of the neighbor on her right.

Her friend, who shall be called Cynthia, was twenty-two, with an M.A. from Columbia and B.A. from City College in New York, a speech therapist, she is the daughter of a New York City police sergeant. She said, "After two-and-a-half years of psychoanalysis, I joined Edgar Cayce. The spirit life is one step beyond analysis. In analysis it is just you and the therapist but there is no reason why. This gives one a purpose."

Leaning forward energetically, Cynthia, who appeared to be the leader of her group, exclaimed, "I was Jewish, but the temple was meaningless. You went to a *bar mitzvah* for the party afterward, or to the temple to meet boys. But in the Group, on the days when we do not meet, we all try to pray simultaneously wherever we are."

PHOENIX

In Scottsdale, Arizona, a suburb of Phoenix, a remarkable film showing the connection between St. John's dreams in the Book of Revelations and the seven glands in our bodies was presented to me in the apartment of Mrs. Erika Bauer, a conversational woman, comfortably built, of medium height who combined sincere dedication with an undertone of sadness that the world would not believe. Mrs. Bauer owns an apartment complex, called the Paradise Gardens, "Where Apartment Living is Fun!" Rent there is four hundred to four hundred and fifty dollars per-unit per-month during the winter and one hundred and fifty dollars in the summer. Sunlight bathed the green grass, the swimming pool, and the neat units.

Mrs. Bauer is a member of the A.R.E. Council in Phoenix. "There are about one thousand members here, two hundred of whom are active in 'Search for God' Groups. A few years ago there were five to seven groups. Now there are thirty.

"I had an uneasy feeling when I rented an apartment to this man and his wife. One afternoon a friend told me the man had come to the office twice. I was afraid something was wrong. I knocked on the door and called twice but the radio was on." The man appeared suddenly and said "I've given my wife instructions to shoot anyone who touches the doorknob." Shaken, Mrs. Bauer related how—back in her apartment—she asked the Father to bless him. She also spoke of how A.R.E. had helped her to "control" herself when several hippies had damaged an apartment she rented to them.

Mrs. Bauer's son, about sixteen, accepted A.R.E. in an offhand eager way. He'd been brought up with it. Although

I arrived unannounced, they talked freely to me, welcomed me into their home, gave me a sandwich lunch and showed me slides with a syncrhonized tape-recorded commentary, as the Phoenix sun crept in through the Venetian blinds.

Later I visited the A.R.E. center in Phoenix which is housed in a slightly rundown frame building. In Phoenix there is also an A.R.E. clinic.

VIRGINIA BEACH

At Virginia Beach, Virginia, the headquarters of A.R.E. are housed in a white clapboard house with a slate-gray roof. With its big Southern porch all around, it looks as if it might have been a bankrupt hotel from the early part of the century or possibly a private house. There was a certain amount of peeling paint on the house exterior. Located as it is in a comfortable middle-class section of the beach-front area where the neon signs are infrequent, there is a slight scent of decay in the air—perhaps from the sea.

Though there were only two or three cars in the public parking area in front of the house, the car space for the employees in the back was filled. At first I noticed several people with slight physical handicaps, which made me wonder about the psychological attractions of A.R.E. but then in the vast office with dozens of secretaries I saw a number of very pretty girls.

The chairman of A.R.E.'s Board is Hugh Lynn Cayce, the son of Edgar. Mr. Cayce looked like a president of the Rotarians or your friendly life-insurance salesman—brown suit, yellow tie, and smoothly-combed white hair. His friendly face surmounted a comfortably-padded body. Mr. Cayce's office furnished with much dark leather looked like that of a prosperous Southern businessman, or even a bank president.

"How does it feel to be the head of a growing . . . movement?" I had hesitated over the word "movement," as Mr. Cayce had told me at great length A.R.E. was not a religion.

"Frightening . . ."

"Why?"

"Well. You have to go back of course to growing up in a family where my father was constantly in the headlines of newspapers all over the place and was now and then being arrested, who was constantly, I knew, in conflict with what he was trying to do—always the question, 'should I be a photographer or should I be a psychic?' . . . running frequently, trying to stop giving readings, then being sought after. . . . After I got out of college I became involved in the organization but there was conflict all the time, constant pressures of all kinds. . . . Harmon Grow in a doctorate described him as a seer in a seerless culture.

"And so having a mass of forty-nine thousand pages, over ten million words, what do you do with them? . . . When I say frightening, it's frightening that I'm going to have to deal with a major movie here very soon on the life of Edgar Cayce. What do you do with hundreds and hundreds of young people who come here and say 'Well, all right, you say "Get off the drugs" where do I go?' What do you give to them? What do you say to them? The responsibility involved in not fooling people. . . . You're sitting on top of a mass of material that people search out and want to touch like magic of some kind, but it's not magic.

"When I say frightening, I mean in a minor sense—of awe at the responsibility of trying to work with a mass of data on one man."

"Are you afraid that the turmoil that surrounded your father's life will be repeated in yours?"

His voice rising, he replied, "Oh, no. One psychic in a family's enough, and you see—without the emotional pressures of a society that attacks the psychic himself—I'm on much more stable ground in that sense. I've tried to be more objective and therefore it's harder to criticize. . . . I have led a pretty reasonably balanced life. Where my father had great difficulty, I have no problem at all in becoming involved in civic affairs, in church activities, in boy scout work for twenty-five years.

"We do a lot of work with doctors—medical research in the readings. A doctor in Phoenix hospital applied this type of treatment to things Edgar Cayce suggested. He then wrote a report—so many improved, so many did not—and delivered it to fifty doctors at a medical conference in Phoenix. It applied to several different kinds of diseases, epilepsy for example.

"We have a medical research division—chiropractic, osteopathic, physio-therapy-massage, sweats, colonics, and whirlpool baths. In the sweats, Cayce suggested that for people with certain arthritic tendencies that if you put certain oils in the water, there would be a helpful absorption through the skin. Physiotherapists such as Dr. Riley have found this to be true. Peanut oil plus mineral oil is effective."

While there, I attended Hugh Lynn's lecture on Christ Consciousness. Among the large proportion of women in the audience of about forty people, there was a long-haired neatly-dressed young man. Several people wore smiles of devotion throughout the speech. Cayce referred to a "visitor married to a Japanese lady, a Presbyterian minister."

Describing himself as "a seeker," Jim, a curly-haired long sideburned young man, smiling pleasantly said, "A.R.E.'s dream interpretation was more complete than that of Ouspensky. [A Russian mathematician and leading disciple of Gurdjieff. See Chapter III.] I was interested in the Gurdjieff-Ouspensky movement previously. For example, I had a cough which would not go away. I dreamt of watering grass with lemon juice. I subsequently drank some lemon juice and my cough disappeared. Reincarnation and karma are helpful as you realize you are a soul who has chosen this life to work out particular problems and that your parents are not to blame." I said I couldn't remember my dreams, and he replied, "People who can't remember their dreams have a tendency usually to be repressed." When I asked him if I could use his name, he spent some ten minutes discussing my request over the phone with Dr. Herbert Puryear, formerly an assistant professor of psychology at

Trinity University, Texas—now evidently Number Two in A.R.E.'s organization.

When I interviewed Dr. Puryear, I found that his first interest was in the one thousand Cayce readings on dreams which are becoming psychologically very popular at the present time. He said, "The Association is dedicated to the idea of developing new concepts from the fact of ESP. Science today refuses to accept ESP despite the body of evidence because it conflicts with their concepts. We are trying to develop new theories.

"A.R.E. is not a religion. There are no dogmas. Edgar Cayce said Jesus was the Master whose teachings one should follow, but this year we sponsored—to the surprise of some of our members—Dr. Rayner Johnson, who said that one should have a spiritual master in the body, and that they could be equally valid in any religion.

"Cayce said there is the spirit, the mind, and the body. The universal spirit is translucent through the seven body glands—pituitary, pineal, thyroid, thymus, adrenal, cells of Leidig, and the gonads. The spirit is unbalanced when one gland dominates the others as when one is angry, such as the adrenals. This is why Cayce recommended about fifteen minutes of meditation every day.

"The reason so many young people are turning to A.R.E. is that they are souls from Atlantis, who had a highly civilized culture like ours, who had no wars, returning into the generation born in about 1943 or 1944 when conditions are similar for working out their karma."

On sex, Cayce's philosophy seemed to be to do what was best for the individual. On war, he apparently advised a peaceful personal approach though not prohibiting those who wanted to fight.

"I receive about fifteen thousand dollars a year," said Dr. Puryear, "considerably less than what I got as a faculty member at Trinity, Texas, where my children would also get free tuition at a college such as Stanford under the exchange free-tuition program for faculty children."

NEW YORK

The Cayce center in New York is at 34 West 35th Street, and there are lectures open to the public every week in the drab Willkie Memorial Hall at 20 West 40th Street. A donation of one dollar and fifty cents is requested. An associate membership costs five dollars. Subjects range from "Emotions and attitudes: hang-ups or opportunities?" to "Politics in Upheaval" to "Edgar Cayce and Judaism." The director, Shane Miller, is a personable man. A lecturer from Adelphi made the mistake of addressing the rather poorly-dressed crowd with words like "theocentric," "anthropocentric" and "ideocentric," producing smiles from two hefty truck-driver types near me. Among the books on sale was one on auras, the colored light emanating from the human body. Cayce could see them. Green means a talent for healing.

The two books particularly recommended by the A.R.E., are *Edgar Cayce—The Sleeping Prophet* by Jess Stearn ("America's Greatest Mystic!" is on the cover) and *There Is a River* by Thomas Sugrue. Some A.R.E. people seemed more enthusiastic about the latter. The Sugrue biography, first published in 1943 (two years before Cayce's death), is really good—timeless, penetrating, and well-written. A more than cursory perusal of the Stearn book (reportedly a best-seller) indicated it to be sensational, with little more value than introducing readers to A.R.E.—unselective, disorganized, and Pollyana-ish in its treatment.

Quotations from *There Is a River*:

"The system of metaphysical thought which emerges from the readings of Edgar Cayce is a Christianized version of the mystery religions of ancient Egypt, Chaldea, Persia, India, and Greece. It fits the figure of Christ into the tradition of one God for all people, and places Him in His proper place, at the apex of the philosophical structure; He is the Capstone of the Pyramid."

One of the more convincing aspects of the Sugrue study are the six case histories of medical readings, the language of which, perhaps because of Cayce's constant lifelong reading of the Bible, is somewhat stilted, and rather technical. He advised treatment of a priest suffering from epilepsy: "We would apply each evening, for two evenings, the heavy Castor Oil Packs, at least three thicknesses of heavy flannel, wrung out in Castor Oil, as hot as the body can stand same, and placed over the lower portion of the liver, gall duct and caecum area, this extending, of course, to the umbilical center." Two years after the onset of the treatment the patient wrote, "Complete cure, as far as I can judge, after the lapse of almost two years."

Stearn's biography devotes considerable space to Cayce's readings on reincarnation, earthquakes, medicine, dreams and "world prophecies." He includes recent research on how some of Cayce's medical discoveries are being verified today and up-to-date events in the lives of people for whom Cayce made predictions.

A third Cayce book, by Hugh Lynn Cayce, *Venture Inward* is a worthwhile, if sometimes boring, book which deals with many occult subjects, gives expert and common-sense advice to beginners who are approaching psychic matters, and recommends meditation as the only real road to salvation.

CHAPTER XVII

Some New Christians and Jews

Accompanying the spectacular rise of new religions among the youth population—the baby boom of the years just after World War II—the traditional religions would not seem to make sense. But some tentative avant-garde developments have brought their challenge within the established beliefs.

The New York Times of March 31, 1970, reported that "373 out of 12,959 Catholic . . . schools closed in 1968 and 1969; that 70,652 religious teachers had decreased by 6160, and that total pupil enrollment had dropped 282,882 from 5,245,909 in 1967 to 1968, and to 4,983,027 in 1968 to 1969." The Associated Press reported the first decline ever in Roman Catholic membership in 1969—"a decrease of 1149 from the year before." Michael Novak in the *Saturday Evening Post*, December, 1968, quoted a source as estimating "that attendance at scheduled Masses in Los Angeles parishes with a high proportion of young adults has fallen off by as much as forty percent in the last six months." *U.S. News and World Report* of March 23, 1970, reported "one estimate" as saying "four percent of all priests in the U.S. are dropping out annually—perhaps two thousand and five hundred Roman Catholic clergymen." *The New York Times* for January 18, 1971, reported a survey of a Notre Dame sociologist saying that one out of four parish priests was considering leaving the priesthood. *U.S. News and World Report* said the Roman Catholic Church experienced less than one percent growth last year—the lowest in twenty-five years.

U.S. News and World Report in one estimate said "three thousand ministers" or "one percent" were quitting each year. Speaking of general church attendance, the magazine cited the Gallup Poll as giving sixty-eight percent as church membership a dozen years ago and sixty-three percent today. Church attendance once a week was considered a more accurate barometer, and "has dropped from a record forty-nine percent in 1958 to forty-five percent at present." *The New York Times* reported in early 1970 that, "Protestant Denominations Cut National Staff as Support Falls." The United Presbyterian Church in the U.S.A. eliminated fifty positions last year and expects to cut one hundred and fifty more in 1970 . . ." William Willoughby, Religious News Editor of *The Washington Evening Star,* said on January 3, 1970, fourteen percent fewer persons attended church at the end of the decade. *Publishers Weekly* of April 20, 1970, reported declining business for religious publishers.

John Cogley, former religion editor of *The New York Times,* in a recent *Times* article, said, "The basic questions are concerned with whether Christian belief and distinctive Christian communities can survive in an age shaped by the scientific mentality." Many new religions tend to synthesize science into religion—in effect smothering the danger of science with an all-encompassing viewpoint which controls and explains science. The customary response of Catholic and Protestant theologians has been to try and accommodate their beliefs to science.

Yet avant-garde changes in Christian and Jewish liturgy and politics have been made in an attempt to hold young members. At the same time completely unrelated innovations have always been made by church radicals and liberals. The following scenes typify the search for a more lively religious role which the new religions have successfully accomplished. To me, these progressive Catholic and Protestant movements, by their uncertainty, their clinging to the past while attempting to venture into something new, demonstrate that they are most alert of the traditional church behavior.

TEXAS EPISCOPAL PENTECOSTALISTS

That same indefinable light I had seen on other young peoples' faces was on Samantha Major's. She was a comfortably constructed girl with a visage such as I imagine Joan of Arc's might have been. "I pray to Jesus at any time during the day and speak in tongues. Sometimes when I'm alone doing housework."

Samantha—one of a group of one hundred and thirty-six, mainly young people—belonged to a Pentecostal Episcopal group which shares all its members' salaries and property, and lives in about a dozen houses scattered around Houston. Another girl with curly rich long auburn hair and a long chin demonstrated a youthful "swoop" of arm and legs in a Jewish folk dance she and others do in a community-run coffee house near the University of Houston. Many of the members were students there.

Though they shared everything, it was not the life of poverty I had always imagined the early communal Christians endured. The Pentecostals lead a middle-class existence of unobtrusive homes, neat living and bedrooms and sufficient food. Lunch consisted of sliced tomatoes, roast beef and peanut-butter sandwiches, and iced tea. "We buy milk at eighty cents a gallon from a dairy herd—non-homogenized, non-pasteurized," said Samantha.

"The cows are registered and inspected," Bill, another young member, said quickly.

"My mother," said Samantha, "says 'Don't you drink milk more than two-days old or you'll get undulant fever.' "

At our group discussion with about eight members present, Walter said, "We're trying to get away from the American idea that love and sex have to go together."

He and a young blond curly-haired minister embraced each other by pressing their chests together, heads side by side, an arm of each clasping the back of the other. "It works fine once you get over your fears," they said.

The middle-aged lawyer, who has a general practice, said, "You can show affection without sex."

"Do you mean," I asked them, "that there is no dating?"

"It's group affection," said the lawyer.

"*Well*," said Walter and Jeff simultaneously.

"What do those 'wells' mean?" but they would not elaborate.

Walter said, "In the coffee house on Friday and Saturday nights everyone works together and people are studying the other nights. There's no time for dating."

When I noted that there were no black or Mexican members, Walter said, "We'll see if we bring peace between the two races when the two cultures meet in our area. So far they have never been able to live together."

Ellery Betts (which is a pseudonym), a crew-cut middle-aged member, said, "Five years ago this area was on the way down. The Negroes were fifteen blocks that way and the Mexican seven blocks the other way. Now we're restoring the neighborhood. That house across the street has been repainted."

They run a clinic in the black district and take in ex-mental patients, alcoholics, and former dope addicts. I was introduced to a pleasant-faced middle-aged woman who had been a schizophrenic.

When I shifted my questions to the current political scene, Walter replied: "You might call our lack of political activity irresponsible." He and the others said they just weren't interested.

"Father Pulkingham [the founder of the experiment] and I traveled all over the country speaking. Fifty percent of our talks were to Roman Catholics. The monasteries and convents are getting rid of their traditions, but then they don't know what to do." In all, he said there were now thirty thousand Roman Catholic Pentecostals—particularly around Notre Dame and Ann Arbor, Michigan. In September, 1970, when I wrote to the Rev. W. Graham Pulkingham to inquire further, he answered, "The community . . . was experimental and being found unsuccessful, was disbanded in July of this year."—Except for Father Pulkingham I have disguised the names of the group and its location.

The Texas experiment in a way paralleled the communes of the new religions, which are of course growing rather than disbanding.

NEW YORK

A service at St. Clement's Episcopal Church in New York may typify new liturgical activities similar to the rituals of some of the new cults. The seventy-six person congregation were mainly in their twenties, thirties, and early forties and seemed to be primarily an artistic-intellectual-political-teaching group.

We ate the pieces of broken bread from a whole-wheat loaf, which represented Christ's body. From a chalice we sipped red wine, which represented his blood. On the altar stage, we sang a song.

The service began with a humorous-looking man, Arthur Knopf, banging away on a piano with one hand and keeping time with the other by beating a stick of wood against the wooden piano top in jazz-band fashion.

They had converted the spacious Gothic interior by building a church-stage above the floor, with offices underneath.

Suddenly in front of the stage, decorated with a poster of Malcolm X, a man appeared in splendid Roman Catholic-type vestments—gold and white. He had thick curly hair and an energetic plumpish face.

"Let us all pray for Cambodia . . ." he said.

We all sang a hymn "dedicated to Richard Nixon."

There were a lot of good-looking young girls in the congregation-audience, sitting on steps. The tight-fitting trousers of the man in front of me were belted so low I could see about an inch of his rump.

The stage play, featuring a German prostitute, an American soldier, and a magazine writer, began with necking and petting.

After the play another bushy-haired man said, "Let us pray for Phil Berrigan who is in prison and Dan Berrigan who's being hunted."

The well-known participation of priests, rabbis, nuns, monks, and ministers in Civil Rights demonstrations and anti-war activity is illustrated by the following quote from *The Nation,* May 4, 1970: "Freedom rides, boycotts, eat-ins, pray-ins, speak-ins, speak-outs, noncooperation, the creation of integrated schools, and of schools for Negroes, civil disobedience in a hundred forms, nonresistance in a thousand." The quote described the nineteenth century Abolitionist movement. In the 1930s *The Commonweal,* the Roman Catholic weekly, was full of liberal distress over the Spanish Civil War. The Negro and Vietnam-inspired activity of the religious is nothing new.

Here is a young couple who, familiar with Eastern religions, rejected them and chose to be Quakers:

Donna and Cliff Laing, twenty and twenty-four, have received mail for their anti-war pacifist views. They live in a conservative middle-income part of Bloomfield, New Jersey. "We've been in every demonstration since 1967. We're sick of them. Each time we say afterward, 'Never again,' but then we do. I have a dent in my head from a policeman's billy club in one opposite the United Nations. Neither Cliff nor I have anyone to talk to at lunchtime at our respective jobs because of our views."

In their inexpensive but neat apartment was a Buddha adorned with beads, including an old rosary.

"The trouble with the Hindu religions," said Cliff as we drove in their small Austin America to the Quaker meeting on a sunny spring Sunday, "is that the Brahmans are the biggest hypocrites of them all with their caste system."

"We're trying out the Friends. We were Presbyterians. So

far we like it," said Donna who was conspicuously pregnant. She had a twinkle in her eyes, peering through thick
rectangular glasses.

PENNSYLVANIA

Only two years old, the Center for Nonviolent Conflict
Resolution at Haverford College aroused "a great deal of
interest," said Dr. Paul Wehr, a sandy-golden haired, attractive man in his early thirties, wearing slacks and light blue
T-shirt, and who seemed a gentle person. "Besides the
seminars on conflict and nonviolence, the Center trains in
nonviolence. Before the big demonstration against the war
in Vietnam, in Washington we held training sessions for two
hundred people in an attempt to keep the protests peaceful
and effective.

"If someone like a Weatherman tries to provoke the police by, say, throwing a rock or calling them 'pigs,' we try to
surround him and thus separate him from the police, and
dissuade him verbally. If he persists, we isolate him from
the nonviolent demonstrators by moving away from him.

"Students were shown, among other techniques, how to
sit down, cover their heads with their arms and draw up
their legs in a fetal position to protect themselves against the
brutal charges of police which sometimes occur during
nonviolent demonstrations.

"The four of us permanently attached to the center are
Quakers or have worked with Quaker organizations for
years. Some of our students work in the inner city, teaching
in slum schools, working with tenant rights, associations,
and trying to bring about nonviolent change through
community organizations. Those working in the surrounding Main Line suburbs help to organize middle-class support groups which will act in behalf of constructive change
in the metropolitan area."

Carl Horne, a friend of Wehr who had been a Haverford
student for two years, dropped into his office to discuss "research I am planning to do on nonviolent national defense

in Czechoslovakia in 1968." Wehr was also interested in similar nonviolent methods of resistance such as shown by the people of Norway and Denmark against the Nazis in the Second World War.

Horne was a handsome, slightly long-haired young man, wearing black-rimmed glasses with a style of gentle, almost hesitant, enthusiasm. "Over a year ago I sent back my draft card and subsequently refused alternative service. I hesitated for a year before that because of fear of jail. But I talked with guys who'd done it and thought about it and realized that prison is a part of society like any other though under restricted conditions and that most guys are never in such things as solitary confinement. I was advised to think of going 'through' prison rather than 'to' prison as a terminal situation. As a Quaker, my beliefs and activities, though separate in a sense, are clearly related."

NEW YORK, LOWER EAST SIDE

The little gathering in the dilapidated store was a far cry from the organized comfort-oriented Roman Catholic Church I had known. Most of the thirty people there were young kids who were scruffily dressed. Somewhere a guitar was playing. A priest came in and squinted at us. The usual anti-draft posters hung all around, plus a color photo of some of the My Lai dead. The service was a bit hesitant, but the readings of war resisters' accounts and Martin Luther King's life were moving; certainly all of this made good sense, although the beauty of the old was absent.

ATLANTA

I was struck by the conviction for civil rights shown by attractive Jean Billingsley, a public relations official for the Southern Christian Leadership Conference. Jean was copper-toned and wore big thin-loop earrings. Several white students and hippies turned up to plan joint student-S.C.L.C. action for the "March Against Repression." It seemed a not very inspiring title, indicative in a strange way of the air of uncertainty about the S.C.L.C. headquarters. "Contributions from whites," said Jean, "have fallen off because of uncertainty about the revolutionary turmoil in the country. They are our main source of support." The only time her voice rose with enthusiasm was when she spoke of "Andy Young's campaign for Congress . . . and Jesse Jackson's 'Operation Breadbasket.'" She was referring to the campaign in Chicago for better employment, housing, and businesses for blacks. She went on: "Jackson obtained much of the financial support from black middle income people in Chicago—the first time this has ever been done. The black middle-class has had money such a short time they don't part with it easily." Chicago is where King had failed in a similar campaign a few years earlier. "Our budget will be well under $500,000 this year and the number of our national staff cut to fifty or seventy-five compared to maybe two-hundred and fifteen when King was alive." She pointed to biblical references used by the S.C.L.C. preachers and said, "They often compare Moses' Promised Land to today's struggle."

Elsewhere in Atlanta, I met a young white student leader who said, "The two names everyone says they don't want when planning a demonstration are Hosea Williams and Ralph Abernathy who talk too long and who are boring."

BOSTON

"What do you do here?" I asked in the Havurat Shalom Community Seminary on a tree-lined street in Somerville, Massachusetts.

"Nothing," said one of the members of the Havurat, as we sat in the kitchen. "We gave classes until recently. The most radical thing we do is dropping out of society and living here. Liturgically we've taken the Torah scroll and put it on a cushion instead of the lectern."

A young man with a short beard said, "I've been writing prayers for the Siddur."

Max Simon, as I shall call him, the only resident of the Havurat house, cooked and did repairs there. He remarked, "The twenty-four members have their main influence by teaching Sunday school in temples and being in various aspects of Jewish education by trying to be more open liturgically, theologically, and radically.

"A group of twelve broke away recently because they said we were complacent. They were going to be radical."

I asked what they had done instead.

"Nothing," was their answer.

Later I heard from an active member of the Seminary, David Roskies, who wrote:

"He [Max Simon] has emigrated to Israel . . . The people you spoke with in the Havurah kitchen have subsequently left the country and hardly participated in our activities while they were here. The Havurah is *not* a drop-out center. All of us are deeply committed to the study and communication of the Jewish tradition. Classes are very much alive. Our experimentation with the liturgy is far more extensive than the "dethroning" of the Torah scroll. Three Havurah members now live in the building proper; everyone else within walking distance. Virtually all members are engaged in graduate study at the university."

CHAPTER **XVIII**

Followers
of Jesus

They were living in a simple house in a Tulsa, Oklahoma, suburb with an A & P down the street and lots of flowers and green trees and shrubs in the neighborhood. They had been given the frame building temporarily rent-free in exchange for painting and repairing it, which they had done, so it looked clean and shiny. They were now looking for a permanent home.

There were about five of them in their early twenties, belonging to the Followers of Jesus, founded by Dom Mark Ryan. The Followers are so Roman Catholic it's almost spooky, but they are not—Roman Catholic, that is. Eight years ago there were none. Now the membership—all full time—is six hundred, growing rapidly, usually graduates of the hippie drug scene, recruited mainly from New York's East Village. Dom Ryan's origins are mysterious, as are the group's beliefs in Advanced Beings, whose identities are— with the exception of St. Peter—secret. Their sacraments are the same as the Roman Catholic church, except for a different interpretation of Confirmation. And, of course, they do not obey the Pope. Now they have spread across the U.S., settling in little groups with their monastic vows, strict views on sex, and emphasis on service to people everywhere particularly other young people—in such unlikely places as Salt Lake City, Utah, and Des Moines, Iowa.

Mary Tanner was once a businesswoman and is now divorced. Her son who suffered from a nervous problem recovered immediately once he was welcomed into a Followers community. She had blonde hair with bangs, and she told me, "We believe in equality for women. But women are not master teachers yet because we have two thousand years of the feminine mystique to get rid of. A woman has never been a priest in two thousand years for that matter. I am one of eight women on the esoteric council, and one of us may become a priest when Dom Ryan says so through revelation. As women, we have to learn that physical beauty is unimportant in comparison to the beauty from the soul. It's very difficult to give up a culture that has made us wear makeup and wigs, taught us how to catch a man, and to put on a painted face every morning.

"Now we can do the same jobs as men—carpentry, painting, even collecting garbage.

"When I was an accountant in a business I had to dress up for the job. A girl can only get a job by the way she looks.

"We all follow the same schedule all over the country. It brings us together. Everywhere at 6:15 P.M. we have communion." Mary is in charge of the brothers and sisters in the Tulsa house.

The two principal publications of the Followers are *The Divine Spectrum* and *Poems of a Believer*, both written by Ryan, though he says *The Divine Spectrum* was revealed to him and therefore he is not the author.

The sweet platitudes of *The Divine Spectrum* may be a substitute for paternal affection. An example from page 232 of the 308-mimeographed pages reads "Why should a God wear armor if he is a great and gentle Force?"

There is also the following notation about a British general: At Quebec "General Wolfe's atmosphere became disquieted. His connection with the Infinite was broken," says Ryan. His "power" over his Army was until then "almost magical," but on the heights above the St. Lawrence River he "fell, never to rise again in the material body as a leader of earth forces on the field of battle." This is almost the only historical reference in the work.

The book concerns the vibrations or emanation which is the electrical method of the Deity communicating with us. There is an uncomplimentary paragraph about the established Christian religion. He accuses church leaders of being mercenary and emphasizing a law that would make the people their slaves.

Ryan's other book, similarly mimeographed for the Order, is a collection titled *Poems of a Believer*. His poetry is guileless and childishly innocent, seeking love, often too simplistic, with a storybook charm where God is all-seeing and sweetly affectionate—a heaven where there is always peace, no wars, filled with mystics, happiness and trust diffusing. The vocabulary could be understood by a fifth grader, and the rhythm is as soothing as a nursery rhyme.

The best poem, titled "The Godly Lover," describes in the first person someone on the prow of a sailing ship, whose heart ceases momentarily, whose soul is surprised, on seeing his friend.

> Climbs the night moon
> Then soul speeds out
> To the friend whom I cherish
> Gliding on the sun's rays
> From Earth to Heaven

The narrator says that neither distance nor endless years—

> Can keep me from my own love's dear caress.
> In the dark of night, I bless
> The dawn, and all the ways of tenderness.

Dom Ryan was a man seventy-five-years-old, bald-headed, who looked like a jovial Santa Claus—stocky. The house in which he lives—apparently also the main house of the Followers—is an ordinary brownstone building next to a gas station near the Bowery. He and his wife, whom he described to me as "Blessed Helen," live on the second floor. In the hall of the ground floor, off which are offices and the parlor, are numerous certificates saying the various young recipients have been ordained as priests. Among them is Dom Ryan's document from a seminary with a name like "Grace and Faith Bible College." The founder's office is decorated in early twentieth-century style—heavy furniture. The rather large room, containing Ryan's solid desk, is well lighted from a number of windows looking out onto the drab Lower East Side streets.

Dom Ryan told me, "Originally there was a group of professional people—ministers, doctors, and psychiatrists— who banded together about eight years ago and discussed the shortcomings of churches, and the way in which the Christian Faith could be brought out and serve some of the needs of the people not as a philosophical thing on Sundays but as working handbook . . . it must correlate and work alongside of Science.

"We disregard the Old Testament with the exception of a couple of chapters in Genesis because that's history . . . the Old Testament is full of the kind of barbarism we want to be rid of in this world."

I said, "And would you care to comment on the aspects of vibration and Godly Emanation which I've read about in your book?"

He replied, "The Godly Emanation was . . . I can't call it my book because I received it as anyone might receive what we call a revelation in meditation. Are you talking about the same thing that a physicist is or a chemist in the laboratory?"

"I'm talking about it in the sense that I thought I read it in your book."

"If you're talking about some phoney baloney why then I'm not accepting it."

"What do you mean by vibrations?" I asked him.

Ryan answered in his tenor pontifically-eerie and friendly voice with its Southern accent, "You see, when you use the word 'vibration' I sense the undertone in your use of the word 'vibration' the same as some of the youngsters on the street who really don't understand this particular thing, but they look at it as some pseudo-situation and that isn't the way we use it."

"Regardless of whether undertones are within me . . ."

"I'm not talking about within you."

"What I'm interested in is what you mean when you use it."

"Well, if you put a reed at the end of a coil and hook it up so that it would vibrate it'll create vibrations, won't it?"

"A reed at the end of a coil?" said I.

"Yes. Your distributor for instance, they used to have an old-fashioned coil which would work, I think it was a single-sided motor. You can use a tuning-fork and produce vibration. It can break a glass if you use the proper pitch of note. This is vibration. It's no different with the way you're spoken to from the heaven or through revelation. It's vibration. There are no two types. There are different cycles or frequencies of vibration."

"So in other words vibration can be on a particular wavelength as a way heaven has of reaching you, or on another wavelength it can be the electrical vibration . . ." I said.

"Electrical vibrations, sound vibrations, light emanations, light frequencies, wavelengths of light. They use it in therapy."

Dom Ryan then refused to tell me whether the Followers differed in any way from Roman Catholicism on the grounds that this might be "taking issue and it is against our law to take issue with a church . . ." He felt that there had been too much criticism of each others' beliefs among churches in the past. Nor would he say whether he had belonged to the Catholic Church or any other religion. However, I did elicit from him, "I am a graduate architect from Washington and Lee University."

I asked him whether he believed in "Advanced Beings and the White Brotherhood," to which he answered, "I have seen them. I have seen some very fine people who've cooperated and worked at different times when I was in need, which is nothing different than what is in the Testament. They are Teachers . . . Great Ones. There's nothing new. It's in the Testament. Some of them have shown themselves on earth to many people." Once again he refused to identify them on the usual grounds that it would "be getting into the field of faith of another person." Some Advanced Beings were on "the earth plane" and some apparently were not.

Dom Ryan said the Followers practiced all of the Sacraments—Baptism, Confession, Communion, Ordination, Marriage, and Extreme Unction—except for Confirmation. "We do not use Confirmation as a singular thing. We use Baptism and it is a Confirmation because originally Baptism and Confirmation were given at the same time, and it was the confirmation of the parent that they would give this person unto Christ as a servant of Christ. Then it was separated later on by some of the churches." Clearly their sacraments are almost exactly the same as those of Roman Catholicism.

"The last rites," he said. ". . . We discourage sadness at this time, as to us it is the birth into a much better life than we are in. Either we have to believe that, or we can't believe the words of Jesus Christ. Say that you are following the teachings of Jesus Christ since you are a Christian, but you'd like to make it in your own way. Well, that doesn't work. That's why so many people have been disappointed in the Christian faith, because somebody has to get their sticky fingers and put their opinion in. If they do things the way the Master taught, why they'll get along all right."

"Why do your followers call you Master Peter?"

He answered it was "just a spiritual thing."

"Do you consider yourself a reincarnation of St. Peter?"

"Well, I think that's everybody's personal opinion."

He explained that there is "a council of priests . . . the esoteric council. We have a corporate structure, which takes care of the business end of things. And of course there's a president, vice-president, secretary, treasurer, and others who are the heads of different departments that are on that board. We have a fellow who's head of public relations and one who is the head of the educational department. They all serve on the board, but they also have their own work to do. They are all young men and women who have taken the vows. They all have to be second-vowed students—in other words, they've taken life vows—and the ones on the council are priests who've taken eternal vows. Outside of that there are no titles. We have those priests who can take over a brother-house—this one or the one at 200 Second Avenue or the one that runs the feeding station where we feed people off the street. We house a certain number of such people and give them clothing. The priest is called the reverend father of the house. The United States is broken up into groups of states, and we call him the apostle head of that state and he's responsible for those groups—missionaries—that are in there. This is done in order to break down the work and to get a more intimate relationship between the brothers and the priests and those that are coming in . . . personal relationships so that everybody is represented. There's no such thing as isolating a brother in South America, and he could still reach the head council here legally according to our laws.

"The final authority on spiritual matters is the council; on business matters it's the board of directors."

He said that he "temporarily" had a veto power on spiritual matters in relation to the council, "but the priests, minister priests, can overrule this by a total vote or the membership can ask for a vote.

"We are welcome at the city prisons. People call us. They like to see us.

"I was born in Michigan, close to Lake Superior and I've been all over . . . my father's gone quite a while ago. He ran a garage, and was somewhat of a machinist and a blacksmith and he bought and sold cars. He was a good man and always treated his family just fine, not a very religious man but he believed in God.

"My wife has two daughters and they're very nice kids."

By the end of our talk his voice had relaxed and had become almost affectionate.

Downstairs I talked with Brother Jones. On his desk was a pamphlet from Vatican II.

"We believe in the Trinity—the triangle—the Father, the Son—like the Sun, the giver of life—and the Spirit which manifests itself in the material. Each is a different personality of God. All of this has been taught to us as a mystery, but in this modern age we must explain the mystery. We teach everything from Vatican II, but we also practice it," said Brother Jones, a well-built young man with brown eyes, dark blond hair and a tanned complexion. He almost always stared at me straight in the eye.

"We are in the Apostolic Succession. Some of the Roman Catholic Bishops are also. It is possible to have the Succession denied, as has actually happened twice. Basically we are Early Christians. We are the Church before the Eastern rite split from Rome.

"I was walking down the street just today and happened to see two black boys lighting a cigarette for a white hippie. 'How nice,' I thought, 'relations between white and black in the East Village are improving.' The moment his cigarette was lit, they smashed him in the face. I ran over to them and the two blacks ran away.

"You won't believe this . . . One of our brothers really liked his possessions—his wristwatch and his hi-fi. He was walking along, and he was held up by three blacks. He gave them an argument. *But they were serious about it.* One of them pulled a gun on him. Two of our brothers were walking back from Lightning [their center in one of the toughest sections of Brooklyn]. Brother Sam stepped in between the black with the gun and the brother they were trying to rob. The black pulled the trigger three times *click-click-click*. There was nothing wrong with the gun. It was loaded."

"To what do you attribute this?" I asked.

"A miracle."

He went on. I looked at his black cross without the figure of Christ on it, and his clerical clothes.

"We've helped calm a number of riots here. In the last one, the Black Panthers—a militant black group—they're a pretty good bunch of guys—asked us to get the white ministers out of there . . . Four of us walked into a crowd. As we approached, everyone yelled for us to stay away. They parted to let us through. It was just like the Red Sea.

"None of us have ever been hurt. We can't be. We're protected. I never worry about what to say, as the Spirit will tell us."

Ryan drove me over to the Lightning Center in the Bedford-Stuyvesant area of New York. The Lightning Center was formerly a bar. A group of men were having their dinner. A black who was drunk staggered in and was given food and then a bed. The men were under the strict command of a Followers' muscular thirty-year-old priest who expertly tossed a Pall Mall cigarette to each of his flock.

After supper Brother Jones came over and spoke enthusiastically of the Spirit, finding oneself, loving God and one's neighbors. Most of the dozen or so students seemed to be in their thirties and early forties. They were a tough but healthy-looking bunch, including one with a big tattoo on his arm, and another, rather dandified, who looked like an ex-alcoholic and who smoked a cheroot. The priest in charge, Brother "Alphonse" [I think this was his name], told me afterward, "All but three of them are under thirty. They've mostly had heavy drug experiences. One was on horse."

South Philadelphia, a neat low-income district, all white:

In their top-fourth-floor apartment was a tall young man. "My name's Brother Malcolm. I dropped out of my Freshman year at Penn State where I was studying photography, after taking acid. My father has a business selling computer services, with two salesmen and two secretaries. He has a big Cadillac. My brother's a rebel, working in draft counseling in San Francisco.

"I was a hippie in Chicago. After I came out of the mental hospital, I started going down again, taking acid, dealing grass, a little sex. It was hell. I was guilty all the time. Several friends and I built a shack on the beach by the

Lake Michigan dunes and for three months we cleansed ourselves, doing Yoga meditation, finally even cutting out grass. We gave all our money and books to the Followers of Jesus. During the day we helped out in the street or we panhandled. We got more money than we needed so we'd buy oranges, twenty for a dollar, and pass them out so it helped feed the street. Then Dom Ryan asked us to join [I had known a girl from the Followers about a year earlier].

"This girl has left the order temporarily because she and a brother at a picnic walked off into the woods. They didn't do anything, but that's not allowed. She was told she'd have to keep silence for three months. I was the cook for five months.

"Ten days ago I was ordered to move to Philadelphia. My family's very happy I'm in the order, after my previous life. We have visions, but I'm not allowed to talk about them except to Brother Superior, not even to a brother, as it might start bad scenes like he'd think 'Why haven't I had one like this.' We get up at 5 A.M. Every other day we have communion. We use matzoh bread and wine. It's transformed into the body and blood of Christ. It's true. We eat it. There's a lot of intense energy."

"What does the service consist of besides the communion?"

"I have a feeling I shouldn't tell you. I can't remember."

"You don't expect me to believe that?"

"It's like in the Bible, 'The wind came to them and they spoke in many languages.' The spirit makes me forget . . .

"I'm much happier now than when I was a hippie . . . Brother Superior and Sister Superior . . . They're married . . . Three evenings a week we have patrols and go out into the streets and help in any way we can." His eyes were blue and seemed glazed. He smiled often. He looked as if he'd been through a shock in the past. He was a tall young man, informally but neatly dressed.

In their living room of their tidy top-floor apartment was

a card table covered over with white cloth, a heavy gold cross, and two candles.

"After a person has taken final vows he cannot leave. We do not prevent him from leaving by force. But he would not benefit spiritually.

"Brother Simon's a janitor. Sister Catherine is a receptionist, Brother Ebenezer works in a record store. Sister Superior's a secretary. Brother Willie has some crazy job or something in an electronics plant. Our vows are Purity, Obedience, Service, Poverty, and Humility.

"If I have sexual temptations, I think of Jesus.

"We follow the teachings of the Master Jesus and basically the four gospels. We are Early Roman Catholic and live for the fundamentals. Most of us are Protestant. A few were originally Roman Catholics. I was Jewish. Brother Superior was ordained by the head of our order in New York by Dom Ryan. Most of the people at our New York center are ex-hippies."

In the office-bedroom Brother Superior and Sister Superior of Philadelphia commune spoke with me.

"I won't tell you the identities of the Advanced Beings, except for St Peter who is one. They belong to the White Brotherhood, which the Masonic Orders and Rosicrucians believe in also.

"A Revelation might tell us to go to the Congo and work there. For a Revelation to be recognized as true, the person who receives it must appear before the esoteric council. If they recognize it from their own visions, and decide it could not have come from the intellect, it will be written down.

"For a brother and sister to make love is a serious offence. Discipline ranges from the maximum which is temporary expulsion from the order, to restriction for, say, a month. The person will be allowed only to go to his job. It is for his good and that of the order. Dating is allowed only by permission when both parties involved have reached self-realization."

So said Brother Superior Hawkins, an auburn-haired, clear-eyed young man wearing clerical collar and suit, white socks and sandals, who is "the Brother Superior" of the Philadelphia Center, and "apostle for the seven Eastern States." His wife, Barbara, is "co-director in charge of the sisters."

The Bible study class was recital and discussion of Matthew, Chapters Thirteen and Fourteen. They laughed and giggled at a joke I found unfunny. Brothers Simon and Malcolm sat opposite the two novices—a young man and woman—who wore ordinary clothes. Brother Superior sat at the head of the kitchen table. Light was supplied by three candles.

"We worship God and God the Father, but not Christ who was a Master and perfect natural man. God the Son and the Holy Spirit are manifestations of God. We are all the Sons of God."

We drove to the center of the bar and striptease section of Philadelphia. Brothers Simon and Malcolm were to go on patrol, offering aid to anyone who needed it.

"Are you tempted by the prostitutes?"

"Nah," laughed Malcolm. "We all pretty much had our fill of free love as hippies."

Brother Simon said, "I haven't seen any violence on the strip in Philadelphia. It's calmer here than in New York."

Note: The name of the above religion is invented, as are the locations, personal characteristics; the quotations from the mimeographed books of poetry and mysticism are fictionalized, as well as the reference to Godly Emanation and to St. Peter. The essential aspects of the "Followers of Jesus"—their ritual, activities and behavior—have been adapted from an existing religious group.

PART VI

Sino-Japanese

CHAPTER **XIX**

Nichiren
Shoshu

"Nam-Myoho-Renge-Kyo" goes the seemingly endless chant. "Nam-Myoho-Renge-Kyo . . ." The beads being rubbed together like gravel. The two actions are central to the Nichiren Shoshu Buddhist religion, founded by Nichiren Daishonin and now containing two hundred thousand members in the U.S. While kneeling, rubbing the beads, and intoning these sacred words, they worship a scroll of paper, called the "Gohonzon."

In Japan this religion is known as Soka Gakkai, which means Value Creation Society. With seven million five hundred thousand families, it even has its own political party, Komeito, which is now the third largest in Japan. Its political activities and conflicts with other Buddhist beliefs have aroused bitter opposition. For all practical purposes it is new in Japan since World War II. In the U.S. it is ten years old.

The atmosphere of the New York headquarters of the Nichiren Shoshu sect is young, cheerful, but tends to be a bit rigid and organized.

At 250 West 57th Street, on the fifth floor, down a series of seedy corridors is the "Kaikan" or meeting place. Inside, during the daytime, are a young Japanese woman secretary-type, a young American-looking boy named Harvey sitting at a typewriter, bookshelves, counter, and a bright sign

MIN-ON, their musical organization. To the left is the private office of Mr. Kenji Sudo, the head of the New York branch. In front is the entrance to the sacred room. One's shoes have to come off. At one end on the immaculately-clean beige carpet is an altar and encased there is the "Gohonzon," the scroll describing the potential of individual human life and the key chant "Nam-Myoho-Renge-Kyo." There is a bowl of fruit—apples and pears—which are eaten by the sect's members after twenty-four hours of honorary duty on the altar. There were a couple of potted plants, helping to make the altar "a nice home," as Harvey put it, for the "Gohonzon."

Harvey, a slight charming Jewish boy, discovered Nichiren Shoshu when "a pretty girl next to me in a class at City College asked me if I would like to come to a meeting. I became so engrossed I forgot about her."

Mr. Sudo appeared to be in his early thirties, smoked a cigarette and had eyes that were sometimes troubled by my questions, but who was pleasant and cooperative. He was neatly dressed in a light blue-gray suit. "We have no rules on sex," he said when we talked about youth, "but if young men and women live together and they wish to become leaders, it may set a bad example. I say, if you live together, you should marry."

I turned to other issues and he answered: "We are for world peace but if a young man opposes the war in Vietnam and is drafted he should go because this is the government's policy, though he must retain his individuality." I learned that Mr. Sudo was also the reporter for the *Seikyo Times* a Soka Gakkai newspaper in Japan, which pays his salary in the U.S.

"Christianity is a gateway to Buddhism," he told me. "But other buddhist sects are heretical and we oppose them strongly." Harvey added, "We have Moslem Buddhists, Jewish Buddhists, Catholic Buddhists . . . What happened to the 'flower children' of Haight-Asbury? They joined Soka Gakkai."

There is much emphasis on wholesome All-American activities such as athletics, fife-and-drum corps, dancing and orchestra.

When I first walked into the office at 7 P.M., on the evening of a service, the first thought that came up from my unconscious was "What's going on here?" On later reflection I was still baffled. Here were Americans—real American-Americans kneeling on the yellowish carpet rubbing beads together with both palms and chanting rhythmically over and over and over, sounds such as "Nam—um—haw—yaw" . . . *for forty-five minutes*, without stopping, except for the very occasional clanging of an Oriental bell. Could it be their way of escaping from their daily New York realities?

There must have been one hundred people packed into the sacred room. After about twenty minutes Sudo came in and led the chanting. I borrowed *The Liturgy of Nichiren Shoshu*, a tiny book. I attempted to follow the endless sound. It was either the repetition of one phrase or rapid chanting of *The Liturgy book*. I was unable to keep up with the latter, nor could I understand it, as it was written in Japanese. The people in the front half of the audience seemed to be participating fully. Some of those in the rear were only mumbling. There were a large number of young people in attendance, a few blacks, middle-to lower-income in appearance. Among the chanters was a beautiful black woman, and a well-dressed businessman. At the end of the chanting, Sudo left. Immediately four girls jumped up and began to sing a patriotic kind of song followed by three cheers. Then the men, all young, arose and making manly fist gestures sang a similar song, ending with three "Hip, hip, hoorays."

Sudo then gave a lecture on Buddha, Nichiren Shoshu, Gautama Buddha, and Lotus Sutra.

Later, I tried again to gain some understanding at a smaller meeting of about ten people in an apartment on New York's West Side. There were several blacks, two Japanese, a well-dressed American businessman, and other Americans present. A senior leader gave a pep-talk on how you could control your environment through Nichiren Shoshu. After the meeting, I spoke with Elena (I've changed her name), who was middle-aged, with a birdlike face, and an expression that reminded me of a little girl. She told me, "I had cancer, had my bladder removed. My kidneys were in bad shape. I was scared and depressed. Then my eighteen-year-old son said, 'Why don't cha try chanting, Mom?' 'Why not?' I thought. A few months later I went to the surgeon and he said, 'You're much better, Elena, but I can't take the credit.' I chant three or four hours a day—in the morning, at noon, in the evening. I do it in the living room on a prayer mat. My husband's a cook and he's often around. We live in a five-room apartment in the Bronx."

PRINCETON

They were very young, sincere and enthusiastic—these two Princeton University undergraduates, a slightly older graduate of Princeton '62, and one from Rutgers.

Alex March (name changed) said, "At first you feel foolish chanting and rubbing beads together. What the hell am I doing? Your head aches and you feel bored after a few minutes. But after a while there is a transformation. You think of everything you want—a new job, a date, a trip. You ask the Gohonzon. It changes your whole life. You cut your hair. Your body is healthier. Everything is seen anew. Colors are fresher. You appreciate the green of tree leaves. If the Gohonzon does not give you what you want, you realize it was something you did not really want anyway, it was unrealistic. Soka Gakkai puts you in touch with real worlds—worlds of yourself, your studies, your girl friend, parents, whatever it is."

They said there were sixty-eight Soka Gakkai undergraduates at Princeton and that there were now one or two or more at every college in New Jersey. The University had offered them a room which next year they expected to use for their meetings.

They conceded that they did not know what the long prayers meant, but this was not important. It was the doing of it, rather than the meaning, that counted—like Mc-Luhan's "The medium is the message."

SANTA MONICA, CALIFORNIA

Dominating the relatively few buildings and beach cottages on the beach front of Santa Monica, California, is a three-story whitewashed brick structure with large black letters painted on the side: NICHIREN SHOSHU OF AMER-ICA. It was built as a National Guard armory. The previous tenant was Syanon, the famous group that cures drug addicts. In October, 1968, Nichiren Shoshu moved in.

"The largest meeting room on the third floor was once a drill hall," I was told by Guy McCloskey, who looked like an ex-halfback with his wide shoulders and muscular body, a former Roman Catholic, now public relations director here. There were the usual Gohonzons, offices, cheery exhortations on walls, the weird sound of two girls chanting. (Were they drowning out of their souls the sickness of Los Angeles? I wondered.)

Mr. M. Kikumura (executive secretary of the U.S. organization) had been an auto mechanic, and had joined the new religion ten years before. As a child he had been imprisoned with his family for four years in Arkansas during the Second World War and the Japanese-American persecution. He referred to his earlier personal troubles, but did not elaborate. He was a strongly-built man, of medium height, slim, with a direct manner.

"Does Nichiren Shoshu plan to enter politics in this country?" I asked.

Kikumura replied, "No. . . . Regarding politics in this country, Professor Sadanaga, the general director of our headquarters in America, has said that Nichiren Shoshu has no reason to be entering politics in the United States. The U.S. already has a government structure of its own. In Japan, Nichiren Shoshu has a political group, Komeito, because naturally with fifteen to twenty million members, there can be a concern for the type of government they have. Thus, in Japan, there is a Komeito Party. In the United States as the membership develops to twenty or even thirty or forty million, there may be one. A member in the Democratic Party might run for Mayor or Governor. It is strictly up to the individual what ticket he would run on under the two-party system we have in the United States"

"Are you saying that in the future if the membership of Nichiren Shoshu increases considerably Nichiren Shoshu will form a political party?"

" 'No, we will not' is the answer that Mr. Sadanaga has given frequently. And from Nichiren Shoshu we cannot tell people to become a doctor or a lawyer or to become a Mayor."

I asked, "Nichiren Shoshu's strong opposition to other Buddhist sects perhaps indicates a religious intolerance which seems incompatible with the American tradition of religious freedom?"

A voice on the building loudspeaker system said, "Dick Sonota, please call the operator, Dick Sonota, please call the operator."

Mr. Kikumura continued, "We might have strong opposition from various other religions. All Buddhism branched out one way or another from Gautama Buddha's about three thousand years ago to the numerous different sects of Buddhism today. And because Nichiren Shoshu is the only Buddhism that practices and propagates the orthodox Buddhism, the Lotus Sutra, naturally there is going to be conflict."

I asked, "Can you give any assurance that the condemnation of other Buddhist beliefs may not be extended to Christianity and Judaism in this country?"

He declared, "I have heard Professor Sadanaga say this conflict will not take place as much as it did with other Buddhist sects. He said in this country there are many different sects of Christianity but in general, the Christian people have not seen God. They're in search of God. Nichiren Shoshu opposes other old Buddhist sects because they have taught the old teaching where they have made statues of Buddha or images of God . . . they worship this idol which they feel is their Buddha.

"When Gohonzon is given to the Christian people, I have heard Professor Sadanaga say, it is as though we have given the Christian people a mirror. 'When the mirror is given,' he says, 'what shall they see?' He says, 'You will see yourself. Nam-Myoho-Renge-Kyo itself is the everyday life —not some saint. No, Nam-Myoho-Renge-Kyo is the every day life of each individual life.' So when you look into the mirror you see yourself. Within yourself is God, or we say, Buddha. The life of Buddha exists within yourself."

"In the book, *Japan's New Buddhism*, there is an extensive description of a highly organized youth demonstration at a big stadium in Japan, and, as you know, authoritarian regimes often have exceedingly well-organized youth movements too. Do you plan to avoid any similarities?"

"We plan to avoid it and wherever we congregate we have no violence. In Nichiren Daishonin's philosophy we find out that worshipping the Gohonzon of people chanting Nam-Myoho-Renge-Kyo regardless of religious background or nationality brings forth the true nature of all men. When you chant Nam-Myoho-Renge-Kyo the various desires or ideals in life and the happiness you seek in life starts growing and developing slowly but surely every day. I do not have to beg you to do good things. It's automatic nature that you will bend over to help a stranger . . . to even take food out of your mouth and give it to somebody that is starving, and if you see somebody in pain to feel really sorry for them and want to comfort them."

"What is the position of the organization if a member proposes changes in the belief or ritual?"

"We accept all constructive thoughts and everybody has the right to give their opinion but we cannot change the statements and the documents and the philosophy which Nichiren Daishonin wrote and practiced and left for us.

Nichiren Daishonin passed away approximately seven hundred years ago."

In *Japan's New Buddhism*, by Kiyoaki Murata, it is pointed out that Soka Gakkai in Japan had 3000 families in 1951, 765,000 at the end of 1957, and 6,876,000 in early 1969. By 1979 this religion plans the conversion of one-third of Japan's population. Nichiren Daishonin's interpretation of Buddhism stresses the practical—what a man can actually do. He advises also that a religion should correspond to the particular country. Mahayana Buddhism and the Lotus Sutra apply to Japan, though Hinayana "might be spread . . . in a country where Buddhism had not been previously introduced." Near Los Angeles, opened in May 1967, is the Myoho-ji temple at Etiwanda. Nichiren said he was Buddha before "the beginning of the eternal past." (See Baba's statements on the beginning of God, Chapter XIV, page 123.)

The founder of the modern Soka Gakkai, Makiguchi, advocated "three values"—Bi (beauty) Ri (gain) and Zen (goodness). The individual was to "benefit" himself and the community. Makiguchi was imprisoned in Japan for his religious beliefs during the World War II and died in jail. Intensive proselytizing is known as "Shakubuku." During the leadership of Toda, who succeeded Makiguchi, there were instances of high-pressure tactics, including the destruction of family ancestral religious tablets by overly enthusiastic disciples, horrifying non-Soka Gakkai members of the same family. The political party of Soka Gakkai believers, Komeito, has said that it is "a synthesis of capitalism and socialism," wants to merge government and Buddhist philosophy, opposes amending "the present pacifist constitution," flatly opposes nuclear weapons, advocates the execution of those who make them, supports the UN and increased trade between Japan and China, favors dissolution "by stages" of "the Japan-United States Security Treaty," wishes for a neutral foreign policy, the development of "a national-guard organization for self-defense" which would eventually "become part of the United Nations police force," and domestically desires "welfare economics."

According to Murata, the author of *Japan's New Buddhism*, President Ikeda is a reasonable, humble, and sensitive leader. Soka Gakkai embodies two precepts of Buddhist theology—*"zuien shinnvo no chi* [wisdom to adapt truth to varying circumstances] and *fuhen shinnvo no ri* [the rationality of immutable truth]."

His book is intelligent, although not stylistically inspired, and very informative concerning Soka Gakkai.

Another book on this religion, *Guide to Buddhism* by Einosuke Akiya, is catechetical, lucid, and boring.

"It follows therefore that man is essentially equal to the Buddha. The only difference, though this is important, is that man inherently possesses the life of the Buddha but leaves it undeveloped while the Buddha has fully developed the Buddha's life, enjoying true happiness."

Buddhism in Japan, according to this author, exists only for "formalities" and "special occasions such as funerals." The young look on it with "contempt." The historical setting is explained in this book. Nichiren Daishonin was about to be beheaded, when suddenly "night became as bright as day." The astonished soldiers abandoned their execution.

In a subsequent persecution three farmers were beheaded, causing Nichiren to decide that the moment had come for him to inscribe "the Dai-Gohonzon."

"By chanting Daimoku ['Nam-Myoho-Renge-Kyo'] to the Gohonzon, a believer will attain the same state of life as the Buddha."

"What does 'Nam-Myoho-Renge-Kyo' mean?"

"First, 'Nam' is a phonetic derivation from the Sanskrit Namas which means 'to devote one's life' to the Buddha. . . . Next, 'Myoho' means the Mystic Law but it eliminates any shade of miracle. It is so-called because the mystery of life is unthinkably profound and therefore is beyond man's comprehension. . . . 'Ho' means law. A familiar law is found in

the growth of man . . . Third, 'Renge' is the law of cause
and effect. . . . Lastly, 'Kyo' . . . means the function and
influence of life."

A third book explaining Soka Gakkai is far better written
than the two mentioned above: *The Complete Works of
Daisaku Ikeda.* It is to a considerable extent history, science, and politics condensed for Soka Gakkai members, as
seen through "true" Buddhism. Ikeda admires English parliamentary democracy, though he neglects to mention the
advantages and disadvantages of the growth of British Im-
perialism which of course accompanied the development of
the parliamentary system. Daisaku Ikeda's historical ac-
curacy may be determined from his assertion that the
growth of Parliament was the result of a parallel rise of
religious consciousness in English life. His examples are
the Wesley Brothers, John Locke, David Hume, Jeremy
Bentham's utilitarianism and Gladstone. The political
parties he admires in modern Europe are "West Germany's
Christian Democratic Union led by [then] Chancellor
Adenauer . . . Belgium's Christian Socialist Party . . .
Italy's Christian Democratic Party . . . and Norway's Christian People's Party." He also has a number of rude things
to say about the liberal and conservative parties in Japan.

Viscount Combermere, who earned his doctorate in
comparative religion at the University of London, comments: "Nichiren [Daishonin—thirteenth century A.D.]
was a dynamic, prophetic figure and although technically
he comes within the field of Japanese Mahayana Buddhism,
his apocalyptic message was quite alien to this tradition.
The Nichiren Shoshu claim to be only the authorized agent
—hence the sole proponent of 'True Buddhism.' They view
Nichiren and not the historical Buddha [Gautama] as the
central figure in Buddhist history."

CHAPTER XX

I Ching

I Ching, the Chinese *Book of Changes*, sheds light on the coin throwers' state of mind. Though it does not represent a religion in itself, as a form of spiritual aid it occupies an equally important place in the hearts of its countless enthusiasts. The theory, illuminated by the great psychoanalyst Carl Jung, is that the psychic state of the coin thrower influences the combination of heads and tails (there are six throws of three pennies), which will then correspond to the appropriate chapter of advice. There are sixty-four such chapters with even more subchapters. A course on the *I Ching* taught "as an instrument of personality transformation" is given by Charles Ponce in New York City and Connecticut, and many have taken it.

Wendy Wyman, eighteen, a freshman at Hofstra, said, "I do *I Ching* because it's a friend. Previously, I went to the Catholic Church, but it's out-of-date—the sermons and this English Mass. My boyfriend was leaving home, and we consulted *I Ching* to see whether to continue our relationship, whether to write each other, and it said, 'Part in a noble way.' " She added with a little grin, "He asked it about me, and it warned, 'She is a bold woman.' "

Sitting cross-legged on the bed in his Greenwich Village apartment, folk-singer Arlo Guthrie told me with conviction in 1969 that *I Ching* advised him to keep in touch with his real goal of creative music. He was not to worry about being temporarily sidetracked by his new movie career and outside business interests.

I Ching, the book, is a charming comfort to thousands of young and middle-aged Americans—usually of artistic nature and who may or may not be politically liberal. In America it began to be popular during the mid-Sixties, though it has been influential in the life of China since before Confucius, who was one of its strongest admirers. It is not a book of fortune-telling, though it is sometimes misused in this way. It is a complex, yet easily consulted, method by which the individual can help to understand his unconscious, his conscious, and the external forces throughout the world, so its adherents say. The *I Ching* says that life is full of changes and tries to show the laws governing them—specifically how the individual can adjust to them.

I Ching is published in several versions. The most authoritative and most popular is the Bollingen edition distributed by Princeton University Press in best-selling editions—to that academic organization's continuing pleased surprise. By early 1969, fifty-one thousand copies at six dollars each had been bought in less than eighteen months. A paperback *I Ching* by John Blofeld is both extravagant in its claims (". . . a key whereby future generations could unlock the secrets of the future . . .") and not considered authoritative. However, it too has sold fifty thousand. Taking into account smaller earlier sales and three other versions, there may be between one hundred thousand and one hundred and fifty thousand copies in the U.S., and—using a common estimate of four readers or users-per-book—up to six hundred thousand followers in America.

Not only the rock-folk singer Arlo Guthrie but numerous other celebrities as well as hordes of hippies and yippies have praised it, as I shall mention later.

How is it played? There are two ways—coins or vegetable-type shoots, known as "yarrow stalks." Most Americans use coins—pennies are the favorite; a "lucky" few have Chinese coins with a hole in the center—"like the old French twenty-franc coin," says the author Ursule Molinaro. Bamboo stalks are used by a New York painter. I have only heard of one person who has actually obtained the yarrow stalk, which grew principally in sacred places in China before Mao Tse-tung's time, and is now banned from the U.S. under the anti-communist trade embargo.

The man or woman consulting the *I Ching* throws three coins six times. Whether the coins fall "heads" or "tails" produces a combination. The collation of the six throwings known as "hexagrams" corresponds to one of sixty-four sections of advice in the book *I Ching*. The person then reads the short chapter, interpreting its meaning in relation to his particular problem, and the book will presumably shed more light on his question. The whole process lasts about five minutes.

The ancient "yarrow stalk" method is more time-consuming. It involves fifty stalks and a complicated method of dividing them into combinations.

Blofeld recommends "an incense-burner," and lying on the floor three times before beginning other rituals. A few people always keep *I Ching* on a shelf which must be above their head. But these incidentals are unusual.

I would not dare to assert that *I Ching* has been scientifically proven, but I would suggest that the reader who wishes to dismiss it as nonsense or absurd should study Jung's Introduction to the Bollingen book. He should consider the theory of opposites in human and natural phenomena. He should weigh the curious relationship to the binary system which is the basis for computers as well as the similarity to the numbers of the atomic table. And then too, for centuries millions of Chinese and other Orientals have found it valuable. The basic question is—is it possible for one's mental state to affect the way coins are thrown? J. H. Rhine, Professor of Parapsychology at Duke University, has shown in thousands of tests that people can guess the identity of a card or a number with a success higher than the laws of averages demand. Were the early Chinese philosophers onto something?

The *I Ching* seems to come from the very early days of mankind and relates to the simplest and most profound aspects of nature. Good and Evil, "Yin" and "Yang" meaning feminine and masculine, Heaven and Earth, the Creative and the Receptive are important ideas in the early *I Ching*. This was connected with the yarrow stalks, some of which were long and some of which were short, and which therefore represented opposites. From this there grew the intricate numerology culminating in the sixty-four "hexagrams" in the book, each of which has six lines, and each line of which can be considered whole or broken in two parts. But so far no one seems able to show satisfactorily the connection between the stalks and lines in the hexagram and the daily forces of life. Perhaps the answer is the Chinese theory that all that happens is interconnected.

According to most experts, the *I Ching* seems to have been written in a very early form about 1000 B.C., though Charles Ponce, an American who wrote the book titled *I Ching: Its Usage and Meaning* says, "Around 500 B.C. was the beginning." The word "I" means "change"—in simplified form. And "Ching" is "the warp of fabric," according to Professor Helmut Wilhelm, an Oriental scholar living in Seattle. One suggestion is that "I" was first a pictogram representing the lizard.

The first author may have been Fu Hsi, a vague historical Chinese personage who lived during the era of hunting, fishing, and primitive cooking. King Wen, the head of a western Chinese state, wrote a substantial part of the *I Ching* around 1200 B.C. He was deposed by the Shangs, but his son, the Lord of Chou, overthrew the Shangs and then added to his father's work.

The last author was Confucius, and his disciples. At seventy the Chinese philosopher supposedly said, "If some years were added to my life, I would give fifty to studying the *I Ching*." Once the book advised him to cut his beard— which did not please him. Another story is that he used *I Ching* so much that on three occasions the leather thongs holding together the tablets on which the book was written, broke.

There is also some evidence that *I Ching* influenced Lao-Tse's philosophy.

The Chou dynasty introduced *I Ching* into the government-run schools after Confucius spread the book's fame. Led by Ch'in Shih Huang Ti (213 B.C.), almost every book except *I Ching* was burned by the authorities. In 140 B.C. all non-Confucian schools were banned from the imperial academy. Professor Helmut Wilhelm (his father played an important role in introducing *I Ching* to the Occident) says "imperial will" made *I Ching* important in Chinese culture. Ironically, one of the attractions of the book is that it shows not only how the individual must submit to the laws of change in himself and the universe but how he can influence his own life and the world. Chinese reformers have used *I Ching* as a weapon against autocratic control.

Like change itself, the interpretations of *I Ching* went through several cycles. In the Han era (206 B.C. to 221 A.D.) the interpretations of *I Ching* were rigid. Then a reformer, one Wang Pi, in the third century swept away this conservative view. He was only twenty-three when he died. His influence lasted for almost six hundred years until the Sung rulers ((960-1227 A.D.) added their own analyses, and the *I Ching* enjoyed a renaissance under the Manchus from 1644 to 1911.

I Ching has played a role in Japan, Korea, and Vietnam. The famous Samurai fighters built some of their military strategy from the *I Ching's* recommendations. Blofeld says that the Japanese naval tactics in World War II were drawn from the book, and they failed in the latter part of the conflict when the generals and admirals disregarded *I Ching*.

Surprisingly *I Ching* seems to have survived under the current Communist regime in China. In the early 1960s, when Mao and other Marxist leaders permitted wider intellectual research, the *I Ching* was studied again enthusiastically. One Kuo Mo-Jo was particularly interested in *I Ching* until he was purged. Professor Wilhelm says that even today *I Ching* is examined "when the rare chance of expression is given."

The first Western contact with the *I Ching* were certain Jesuit missionaries who tried to synthesize Roman Catholic theology and Confucian teachings. (Thanks to the Jesuits, the German philosopher and mathematician, Leibniz, who lived from 1646-1716, drew a fascinating parallel between the *I Ching*'s hexagrams and his own binary system.) This was frowned upon by Rome and all of them were later regarded as either heretics or mad. Stemming from this Christian incursion came the initial translation. It was translated in Latin by a priest, P. Regis, and other clergy at the beginning of the eighteenth century.

And there *I Ching* lay until a Frenchman, Jules Mohl, translated it in 1834. The first English version was done by the Reverend Canon McClatchie, M.A., who brought out an imaginative but inaccurate edition in 1876 in Shanghai. More reputable was James Legge's translation in 1882, published in England.

But the *I Ching* remained unknown in the West except to savants. Then Professor Richard Wilhelm, who lived for years in China, published the first translation that was both academically accurate and readable to the layman. He had been advised by a Chinese sage, Lao Nai Hsuan, and had personally practiced the oracle (unlike Legge, who never tested the *I Ching*). An American, Cary F. Baynes of Morris, Connecticut, translated this German version into English.

Jung's prestige undoubtedly has helped spread the *I Ching* in America and Europe. A delightful story relates how he first asked *I Ching* whether he should write the forward introduction to Wilhelm's translation and what *I Ching* thought of his action. *I Ching* answered with hexagram fifty "The Caldron," saying in effect it was full of nourishment. It warned, however (in hexagram thirty-five,

"Chin," which stemmed from fifty) that acceptance in the American book market would be slow. As Jung wrote his introduction in 1949 this prophecy has proven correct. Near the end of his writing the introduction, Jung asked the *I Ching* to comment on the introduction. The response: hexagram twenty-nine, "The Abysmal," which pointed out that Jung was wise to write only an introduction to such a controversial book to Europeans and Americans. The fourth hexagram, forty-eight, "The Well," said that though the task was dangerous the *I Ching* was like an old well that once repaired could be useful. Jung observes that if someone had given him such answers, "I should, as a psychiatrist, have had to pronounce him of sound mind, at least on the basis of the material presented."

The *I Ching* popped up in out-of-the-way Western circles. In 1943 during the Japanese occupation of Peking, Richard Wilhelm's son Helmut addressed a group of Germans on the *I Ching* in the home of Wilhelm Maas. These were Germans who avoided the activities of the German community there. His comments were published in a scholarly and, I think, valuable little work called *Change: Eight Lectures on the I Ching*, which continues to sell at the modest rate of one thousand copies a year, as the bigger Bollingen did until lightning struck in the form of the hippie movement.

From 1949 to 1967, as *I Ching* had predicted to Jung, the book sold about one thousand copies a year. But intellectual and artistic forces were brewing elsewhere. The novelist, Jack Kerouac, leader of the "beat" generation in the 1950s, was intrigued by the Orient. By the 1960s the poet Allen Ginsberg and the drug-guru Timothy Leary were actively encouraging the search into the East. The poet John Cage is said to have taken up *I Ching*, as did some of the Black Mountain School of poets. The currently youthful Tom Wolfe wrote of *I Ching*'s role in the life of Ken Kesey, author of *One Flew Over the Cuckoo's Nest*, and the Pranksters. *I Ching* was consulted in the Pranksters' merry trip across the U.S. And simultaneously the hippies were appearing with their emphasis on universal love and spiritual peace. The *I Ching* teacher Charles Ponce credits the psychedelic painters with first stimulating interest in it.

Things had reached the stage where it may have only taken one small catalyst. According to the sales manager of the Princeton University Press, this was an interview with Bob Dylan, who praised *I Ching*. Dylan, of course, was widely known and respected by thousands of hippies and others who were friendly to them. The sales of the Bollingen book shot up.

Says Abbot Friedland, the sales manager, "One of my salesmen came to me with an order for one thousand books from an incense store in the Village. I said to him, 'You'd better get a check for half the cost from it before delivery,' never thinking the shop could do it. A few days later he gave me the check. So I said, 'I am curious about this. It's a special event. So I'll come along with you when we deliver them.' After we parked our car, the word went up and down the street that 'the *I Ching's* are here' and a number of young people helped us unload the boxes. There was scarcely room for them in the incense shop. Within half an hour the owner had sold a hundred."

Ursule Molinaro was encouraged by *I Ching* in her hope that her latest novel, *Sounds of a Drunken Summer* in which there are several references to *I Ching*, would be bought for films. She is a pretty woman, middle-aged, who lives in a one-room garden apartment on New York's Fifteenth Street with her two cats. She is originally French, and the day I interviewed her she was dressed entirely in black—black shoes, stockings, dress, hat, sunglasses, black shiny coat, and long black fingernails.

"I first became interested in *I Ching* seven years ago. I almost live by the *I Ching*. I use Chinese coins, and cast them on my bed—sometime on the orange Arab bed-cover or on the sheets which often have cat's paws across them. I prefer to get 'Peace' which is eleven . . .

"I asked twice about the film deal. The first time I got

forty-five which is 'Massing.' I took this to mean the masses, the crowd, the public, and I thought, 'Well, I'm sure it will, probably it's going to come through.' A week or two later I asked again. I got 'Abundance, Biting Through.' This is interesting because my style is not quite the usual American style. So I think 'Biting Through' might be my style biting through to the public. The oracle went on to speak of lawsuits. Many films start with lawsuits."

Psychoanalysts, who use Carl Jung's methods, sometimes employ the *I Ching* in their sessions with patients. One patient was George, a pseudonym, whom I discovered to be a twenty-five year-old man with light blond hair, a soft way of speaking. He says, "*I Ching* was useful in helping me to accept the value of the feminine in myself. By using *I Ching* and through the aid of my analyst I realized why society overemphasizes the masculine. It was all right for me to cry, to be sincere."

Another one whom I interviewed, is a slim fine-featured man, whom I will call Terence. He was casually dressed in tan windbreaker, red bell-bottom trousers and blue sports shirt.

He said, "We were out at the beach. A beautiful day. It was at Riis Park on Long Island. My friend's about the same age as me. He's white. His main job is as a free-lance photographer and he's also working now in the theatre of the ridiculous.

"He wanted to go to bed with me, and—you know, I like him very much, he's a very close friend—I said, 'Ask *I Ching*. If *I Ching* says yes, we'll go to bed. If *I Ching* says no, we won't,' and so he tossed the coins on the blanket out at the beach and asked *I Ching*. I would have been in a bit of a jam if *I Ching* said yes and I knew I didn't want to go to bed with him. Like he was willing to put up with me to go through with *I Ching*, because he knew I was very caught up in it at that moment. He was only a halfway believer of *I Ching*. I was concentrating because I knew I didn't want to do it. And he was concentrating too. When I got the answer, I felt fairly relieved. *I Ching* said 'Lead to disaster' and so we didn't do it.

"I've always sort of lorded it over him since then. Whenever he brings it back up, I say, 'Well, you know what *I Ching* said. We can't do that.' If it had come up with the opposite answer, I think I would have tried to get out of it in some way.

"I'm twenty-six—half-Chinese and half-black. I work as a consultant computer programmer. When I first got *I Ching*, I took it to the office where I was working at that time, and we just sat around the office playing all sorts of games with *I Ching*. It was really strange because some girl there was asking *I Ching* questions about her life. She was planning to get married and *I Ching* kept giving her all these dire warnings and like if she got married, it was all right but like she would lose the child that was due and it sort of scared everyone at the office.

"We played all sorts of games—like 'Should I go to lunch at, you know, Tom Jones today or should I diet?'—things like that, but after that week because like a few people would ask it serious questions and because of—I don't know —maybe it was just playing with the *I Ching* and having certain things work out badly. No one at the office wanted to play with *I Ching* after that week.

"I started *I Ching* about two years ago. I read the Jung introduction and I've always been interested in Far Eastern religions and so I decided to see what *I Ching* was like. Fortunately I have a friend, a girl, a major in Far Eastern religions, and she knew how to use it, and she taught me how."

Arlo Guthrie told me about *I Ching* in his two-room apartment on West Eighth Street in Greenwich Village. In the front room were a group of his friends—young, usually with long hair, and dressed in blue jeans. He sat on his bed in the rear room. He is slight of build with a mass of curly hair and looks out at one with the innocence of a chipmunk and the wisdom of a sage—in his handsome twenty-year-old face.

" . . . it seems to me I sometimes use it a lot. I was curious as to where I was going because of these outside interests. I've been investing in this cattle business. I guess they're ranches. I never saw them or anything. I just know I own them. It's strange being a vegetarian, but I think it's better that way. I'll just have to work it out, you know. These investments have tax advantages so that the government doesn't get the money for the Vietnam war. Another interest is the movie *Alice's Restaurant* . . . but I just don't want to be an actor. [He was working on the film's music at the time of the interview.] . . . The hexagram I threw last night changed to sixty-two. [He went into the next room and returned with the Bollingen book.] The first one I threw was thirty-six—'Darkening of the Light.' It refers to times when the change would be into a time of darkness or with bad influences, going down and basically staying to truths, to stay reasonably cool in that to keep your eye on the light but don't necessarily show it, and then eventually come into the light.

"I usually prefer to throw the coins alone . . . I usually hold the pennies cupped in both hands . . . Most of my friends—of the same age— are interested in it . . . or know about it, or are involved with it, somehow or other . . . *I Ching* ties in with the openness of my generation which wants to get the world straight, and have it straight so that we can enjoy it and plan it instead of—as in the past—where parents were always saying, 'We made the world for you.' . . .

"I think I'm beginning to recognize my life as it is now—in relation to where it's going and where it's been, and that's why I'm interested in *I Ching*, because that's what the *I Ching*'s interested in—personal directions. Doing *I Ching* is just another trip. If you realize that, I think it's helpful, because then when you're doing it, you're doing it because you know where it's at, or from your point of view you know where it's at—you might not know what it is but you know that it's only a place, you know, it's not the end because when you get to the end there are no questions, and no doubts and no answers either. So it's not too bad that people play with it because people are playing with it at different levels. We're all doing the same game, but what I was implying was that people should get into one thing— as far as they can get through it and understand all the things on that level that are similar. That's the thing they should do and if they want to do it through the *I Ching* that's fine or if you want to do it through Tarot or if you want to do it through numerology or astrology or through science in general. . . .

"In this time when we are rejecting some things and not others we have to be aware of the good things to reject or to take, you know, whatever comes, and the *I Ching* helps in that way in the sense that it's aware of changes as they occur."

CHAPTER XXI

Zen

"You and your wife should take the hot bath, considering the outrageous price we're charging you," said Jim Lake (not his real name), the slightly unshaven monk at Zen Mountain Center, which was not on a mountain but at the bottom of one, in a valley near Carmel, California.

We had driven over a tortuous fourteen-mile mountain road, rising to five thousand feet, expecting from the brochure and the thirty-eight-dollars-a-night price at least a beautiful view, comfortable rooms, quiet monks, and long shadows. Instead, as we tumbled down the dusty trail into the ex-health resort-camp I was reminded of a mixture of Tobacco Road, hippiedom, and Zen. Which element was triumphing seemed uncertain. We were late for dinner.

"Have some more spaghetti and meatballs," said the young Zen student mockingly to my wife, lifting some limp cold strands with a fork from the side of the jar. Opposite us another student was flirting with a very young girl about nine years old who had long flaxen hair.

I was given a tour of the baths. A naked young man, was sinking and smiling back into the hot waters of a large health bath. Next door in a smaller room lit by a kerosene lamp, two men were standing naked in a bath. One was shaving the other's head—soapy blobs of hair being removed.

"Don't take the lamp. He'll cut my head open," said one bather to the monk with me.

On the wall was a legend about an Indian Chief who ruled the world under the protection of the Sun Deity and had among his other great talents the ability to see the grass grow. He also had a sister, who fell ill. He called in all the medicine men who searched far and wide for a herb, but none of them worked. Finally the Chief decided to take his sister to the Great Pacific Ocean, but before they got there she became so ill they had to stop. She was dying. The Chief fell to his knees pledging his life to God if the girl was saved. Suddenly his body stiffened, turned into stone, and warm golden tears flowed from it. The sister lived and thus Tassajara Hot Springs came into being—the site of the Zen monastery.

There was a smell. Sulphur?

"It's like excrement," I said to my wife, as we went to bed by kerosene light, the lights not working due to the absence of electricity. The hot water—under the previous owner—had long since ceased to work.

From outside came the sound of a rushing stream. Towering above us were the trees soaring up the almost-parched mountainside. There were thick swarms of flies.

The next morning the grinning monk informed me, "The Zen master cannot see you till tomorrow. He is busy today."

"You told me over the long distance telephone you were ninety-nine percent sure he could see me today. At thirty-eight dollars a night we're leaving."

A few minutes later, having just passed by the trash dump fifty yards from the camp, I was approached by the Zen master, a tiny smiling man, and the guestmaster, Stan White, a charming middle-aged man. "Master Suzuki can see you after all today." We agreed on a different price.

Master Suzuki Roshi was an elderly man who used a Japanese fan, sometimes rubbed a white pebble between his fingers, and who once killed a fly and then brushed it gently away with his hand.

He said, "I came to San Francisco in 1959. My first young person was a girl who turned up and said, 'My husband wants to go to Japan to study Zen.' I replied, 'Instead he should stay here and see me. Why don't you study too?' She did. After a week or two the husband turned up, running into his wife—'What are you doing here?' So he started with me, and stayed with his wife in this country. His name was McNair, though eventually he left Zen.

"I came here because the Japanese are more interested in the social side of Zen at the Temple than Zazen. They come to the temple only if you give them food and have a Zen Party."

"What is the purpose of Zen?" I asked.

The Zen master shrugged his shoulders, spreading both palms up, and smiled.

In the office were Lewis and Amy Richmond; Lewis was Harvard '67. They had been at the Zen Center for months.

"We have come closer together since starting Zen," said Amy, who had expressive eyes.

Lewis said, "We will probably stay in Zen for the rest of our lives, but it is uncertain. This is a new thing we are developing here."

Amy smiled, "Sometimes I dream of an apartment and a job . . . but I prefer to stay here."

The Zendo was immaculate. There were about twelve students. They chanted. A drum was struck noisily. An elaborate meal ceremony was performed while two filmmakers with long hair and stained T-shirts moved up and down the aisle, photographing the mostly-young monks and nuns.

There are perhaps about two thousand (estimating very roughly) people, usually young, who practice Zen in the U.S. Zen centers—besides Zen Mountain Center, San Francisco (the biggest)—are in Los Altos, San Diego, Philadelphia, Rochester, Maine, Los Angeles, Los Gatos, California, Chicago, Washington, D.C., Honolulu, Seattle, two in New York City and Mill Valley, and Berkeley, California.

Zen is a puzzle—deliberately so. Its influence, spread by artists and intellectuals, originally taken up by the "Beat" poets of the Fifties, is greater than its numbers.

A learned very well-written book, *The Religions of Man,* by Huston Smith, contains an excellent description of Buddha's life. A short pamphlet, *The Way of Zazen,* by Roshi Rindo Fujimoto, published by the Cambridge (Massachusetts) Buddhist Association, is relatively well-written and lucid, more than can be said for *The Essentials of Zen Buddhism,* an anthology of the writings of Daisetz T. Suzuki (regarded as the leading scholar to introduce Zen to the West). *Zazen* informs us that, "In Japanese Zen today, there are three schools: Rinzai, Soto, and Obaku," describing among other aspects the variations in pain. The goal is "Satori"—a sort of blinding flash of enlightenment. Zen is a mass of paradoxes—all is nothing, all is everything— peace, acceptance of the world—morality can be interpreted in every way imaginable.

"Shimano's zen is heavy," said the girl at the California Zen Mountain Center. She was referring to The Zen Studies Society and its Zendo at 223 East 67th Street in New York City run by the Reverend Eido Tai Shimano, known as "Ty-san."

One of Shimano's students, Peter Gamby, intrigued me. "I was making twenty-five thousand dollars a year as a trader for an investment company, buying and selling the company's shares and getting a commission on the profits. It was a complicated game, like chess, but there were a lot of things on Wall Street I didn't like. I guess I had guilt feelings. I guess if I was more advanced in Zen I could bring Zen and Wall Street together in my life, but finally I decided I'd better opt for Zen at the moment.

"I drove a cab for a year as it was the sort of romantic thing I'd always wanted to do. It surprised my friends, as does my present life. I have a girl friend whom I see one or two nights a week." He sat in the half-Lotus position, had a small beard and a goatee and looked like a young wise-old monkey. He was a Cornell graduate.

Another of Shimano's students is a seventy-year-old lady,

an ex-dancer, who lives with her husband, presumably a tycoon, on a high floor of one of New York's newest, most expensive apartment buildings. Inside it is like another world. The air seems clean. It is completely sealed off from the outside world by steel, glass, and doormen, and there, twenty-or-so stories above the East River and the East Side Highway, you can see below what looks like the contours of another planet, with not a sound to be heard from that noisy road. Feeling like a space traveler, I watched her perform a Japanese tea ceremony—seriously and gracefully—a small woman with large breasts she seemed almost hidden by a floor-length gown as she knelt in her Oriental drawing room, her gray hair impeccably done, the makeup gentle with color. At one point she sat, presumably, in the Lotus position. She spends up to twelve hours some days chanting at the Zen Center. She said: "Doing a Japanese bow, if you are both trained in Zen, with a man you are just meeting, he bowing to you, brings you closer in spirit than if you were lying in bed kissing him."

How does one define so amorphous a group (even the word "group" is too precise) as the listeners of Michio Kushi, a lecturer on macrobiotic diets and general methods of eating the right kinds of food—spiritually and physically. Mr. Kushi, thin ascetic-looking, middle-aged Oriental, dressed in a conservative three-piece blue suit, is a follower, according to his friend Tony Abruzzo, of the late George Ohsawa who died from poisoning himself accidentally while trying to invent a healthful substitute for Coca-Cola and other soft drinks. Mr. Abruzzo said his own ideas and those of Mr. Kushi were related to "Zen Buddhism. Monks at Zen monasteries eat this way and still do."

In the lecture room in New York there were about a hundred people—mainly young and fairly-artistic types plus some middle-aged people, including housewives. Mr. Kushi is a full-time lecturer traveling across the nation. Mr. Abruzzo, a pleasant painter who lives in Brooklyn, counted up the two dollar entrance fees collected by a dark-haired young hippie-type.

Distributed at the door, was a brochure listing "The

Order of the Universe Publications," among which are *Tao Teh King* by Lao Tzu, *The Bhagavad Gita, The Book of Judgment* (The Philosophy of Oriental Medicine) by George Ohsawa, *Chinese Acupuncture* and *Erewhon* and *Erewhon Revisited* by Samuel Butler.

Some of these same people who were attending the lecture also go to a Yoga-like "Awosting Retreat" near Lake Minnewaska in upstate New York, described in a publicity sheet as a place where "Peace, Quiet, Natural beauty is everywhere—sparking waterfalls, cascading brooks, majestic cliffs, wind-twisted pines, and three jewel-toned lakes.

Bibliography

PART I A VARIETY OF RELIGIOUS JOURNEYS

Chapter II   Baha"i'

The Seven Valleys and *The Four Valleys,* Baha"u'lla'h, Baha"i' Publishing Trust.
The Hidden Words of Baha'u'lla'h, Baha"i' Publishing Trust.
The Divine Art of Living, Selections from Writings of Baha"u'lla'h and 'Abdu'l-Baha', Baha"i' Publishing Trust.

Chapter III   Gurdjieff

Beelzebub's Tales to His Grandson, Gurdjieff, Dutton.
Meetings with Remarkable Men, Gurdjieff, Dutton.

Chapter IV   Subud

The New Religions, Jacob Needleman, Doubleday.

Chapter V   Scientology

The Fundamentals of Thought, L. Ron Hubbard, The Publications Organization World Wide, The Church of Scientology of California.
Dianetics, L. Ron Hubbard, Paperback Library.

Chapter VII   Religious Communes

"The Mystical Experience and the Mystical Commune" by Stanley Krippner, Ph.D., and Don Fersh, in *The Modern Utopian*, Berkeley, Calif.

Chapter VIII   Black Muslims

"Elijah Muhammad," by H. J. Massaquoi, in *Ebony*, August 1970.
The Black Muslims in America, C. Eric Lincoln, Beacon Press.
The Autobiography of Malcolm X, Alex Haley, collaborator, Grove Press.
The Fire Next Time, James Baldwin, Dell.

Chapter IX   Witchcraft

The Truth about Witchcraft, Hans Holzer, Doubleday.
The God of Witches, by Margaret A. Murray, Background Books.
Witchcraft Today, Gerald B. Gardner, Citadel.

PART II   THE INDIAN RELIGIONS

Chapter XI   Transcendental Meditation: The Spiritual Regeneration Movement

The Science of Being and Art of Living, Maharishi Mahesh Yogi, International SRM Publications.

Chapter XII   Yoga

Bliss Divine, Sivananda, Divine Life Trust Society.
How to Know God, The Yoga Aphorisms of Patanjali, co-translated by Christopher Isherwood and Swami Prabhavananda, Vedanta Press, Hollywood, Calif.
Raja Yoga, Swami Vivekananda, New York Ramakrishna-Vivekananda Center.

Chapter XIII   Hare Krishna

Kṛṣṇa Consciousness, A. C. Bhaktivedanta Swami, Iskcon Press.
Easy Journey to Other Planets, A. C. Bhaktivedanta Swami, Iskcon Press.
Kṛṣṇa, The Reservoir of Pleasure and other essays. A. C. Bhaktivedanta Swami, Iskcon Press.
The Teachings of Lord Chaitanya, A. C. Bhaktivedanta Swami, Iskcon Press.

Chapter XIV Meher Baba

God Speaks, Meher Baba, Dodd Mead.
Discourses, Volume I, Meher Baba, Sufism Reoriented, San Francisco, Calif.

PART III AVANT-GARDE CHRISTIAN AND JEW

Chapter XV The Process Church

So Be It, The Process Church of the Final Judgment.
If A Man Asks, Robert DeGrimston, The Process Church of the Final Judgment.

Chapter XVI A.R.E. The Association for Research and Enlightenment

There is a River, Thomas Sugrue, Holt Rinehart and Winston.
Edgar Cayce, The Sleeping Prophet, Jess Stearn, Bantam Books.
Venture Inward, Hugh Lynn Cayce, Paperback Library.

PART IV SINO-JAPANESE

Chapter XIX Nichiren Shoshu

Japan's New Buddhism, An Objective Account of Soka Gakkai, Kiyoaki Murata, Walker/Weatherhill.
Guide to Buddhism, Einosuke Akiya, The Seikyo Press, Tokyo.
Complete Works of Daisaku Ikeda, Volume 1, The Seikyo Press, Tokyo.

Chapter XX I Ching

I Ching, Bollingen edition, foreword by Carl Jung, Princeton University Press.
I Ching, John Blofeld, Dutton.
Change: Eight Lectures on the I Ching, Helmut Wilhelm, Bollingen Series LXII, Pantheon

Chapter XXI   Zen

The Religions of Man, Huston Smith, Harper and Row.
The Way of Zazen, Roshi Rindo Fujimoto, Cambridge (Mass.) Buddhist Association.
The Essentials of Zen Buddhism, Daisetz T. Suzuki.